The Sending Church Defined

Zach Bradley
The Upstream Collective

About the Author

Zach Bradley serves as a missions pastor at Sojourn Community Church and a writer for The Upstream Collective. He was formerly a church planter with the International Mission Board before moving to Louisville, Kentucky with his wife, Morgan, and daughter, Alem. He writes at artoflonging.com and theupstreamcollective.org.

Rodney Calfee, the Upstream Collective, Editor.

Contents

Preface
Rodney Calfee

You keep using that word. I do not think it means what you think it means.

Inigo Montoya, *The Princess Bride*[1]

Inconceivable, no? That we could say the same words but mean something completely different by them. But we do. A lot. Language is important, as The Upstream Collective[2] has often said before. It is not just the words we use that are important, but how we use them and what we mean by them when we do. And though many people use the same word(s), we've found that they often do not mean the same thing by them.

We at The Upstream Collective are proponents of the centrality of the local church in sending. If you've followed our blog or heard us speak or spent time with any of us talking mission, no doubt you've heard just that at some point. We, along with LifePoint Church[3] in Smyrna, TN created a forum to deepen the sending church conversation a few years back by drawing practitioners together around the table. We've begun cohorts and discussions and written and taught extensively on the subject. We believe deeply in the Sending Church-but maybe not in the same way others do.

1

Other people and organizations use the words "sending church" to describe what they personally believe and/or do; these are not words that we invented nor an idea new to the mission world via Upstream (actually, we believe the ideas are ancient, stemming from the early church). Many of those churches, however, that would label themselves sending churches, alas, we would not. As a result, though we use common language, we misunderstand one another and the conversation is confused. The waters are muddied.

It is time for clarity. For the past several years, we have had the privilege of partnering with a number of churches that we consider sending churches. As a part of the Sending Church Gathering[4] in September 2013, we asked those churches to define what it meant to be a sending church. Over the months since that time, we have been honing and shaping that definition together and we'd like to offer it here now to clarify what "Upstream" churches mean when using the words.

The definition itself is made up of other deliberate words that also require "unpacking." To that end, we blogged through it almost word-for-word and idea-for-idea from January to September 2014. This book is the result of that work. We mean something specific by the "Sending Church," and we want to help churches see its importance. The beginning point in the dialogue is simply understanding one another.

2

Now, just so you know, we understand that this definition is a terrible run-on sentence. Even so, here it is, the first building block in our conversation:

A Sending Church is a local community of Christ-followers who have made a covenant together to be prayerful, deliberate, and proactive in developing, commissioning, and sending their own members both locally and globally, often in partnership with other churches or agencies, and continuing to encourage, support, and advocate for them while making disciples cross-culturally.

[1] *The Princess Bride*. Directed by Rob Reiner. USA: Acts III Communications, 1987.
[2] theupstreamcollective.org
[3] lifepointchurch.org
[4] sendingchurchgathering.com

Introduction
Zach Bradley*

Purpose-driven church. Simple church. Organic church. Missional church. Deep church. Radical church. Transformational church. Total church. Sticky church. Tribal church. Mission-shaped church. Center church. Vertical church. Everyday church. Deliberate church. Gospel-centered church.

Do we really need one more _____ church?

Yes. At least, we think so. And by that we mean the collective of churches around the world who have recognized that they can no longer forsake their birthright and identity as the leaders in the Great Commission. So at Upstream we're happy to share what those churches are saying and doing. That's where the definition came from. That's where it's being lived out. As you dig into it, here are a few things that might be encouraging to know.

The heart, lens, and experience behind this text are rooted in two places: the global mission field and the local church. Before coming on staff at Sojourn Community Church, I served with one of their teams in partnership with the International Mission Board, where we not only experienced a great multiplication of disciples and churches, but also the realities of the church-agency-missionary relationship from a field perspective. In contrast, over the past few years I have tasted firsthand the joys and challenges of serving as a leader in a sending church. My words are far from my experience alone, but were influenced through and through by numerous great leaders, namely missionary Paul Athanasius*, missions pastor Nathan Garth*, pastor Daniel Montgomery, professor Jeff Walters, and Upstream missiologists Larry McCrary, Caleb Crider, and Rodney Calfee.

In addition, this content originally appeared as a blog project on our website, theupstreamcollective.org, which explains a couple things. First, the mini-chapters are broad introductions to massive topics. But hopefully that means they're accessible, especially for leaders just getting used to seeing themselves as part of a sending church. Second, you'll notice pretty quickly a huge bibliography for such a small book. That's because there's been much written on the different elements of sending churches—but it takes some digging. So we did the digging for you. We also did this so that, if nothing else, you can use the book as a platform for jumping into some of the really helpful resources that are out there.[1]

Finally, we made a choice from the beginning to stick closer to identity and concepts than application and strategy. We know that ideas can be idealistic. The truth is that implementing them will be extremely challenging in some ways. But that's why the conversation is rooted in who we are in Christ, which gives birth to what we do through Christ. We also avoided strategy so as not to perpetuate the very paradigm we're hoping to see reverse: organizations telling churches specifically how to step into mission. Only you, guided by the Scriptures, empowered by the Holy Spirit, and unified in the body of Christ, can decide what being a sending church looks like in your context.

My desire and prayer throughout this project has been simply to encourage churches toward their Savior and his mission. I say expectantly with the author of Hebrews, "Now may the God of peace who brought again from the dead our Lord Jesus, the great shepherd of the sheep, by the blood of the eternal covenant, equip you with everything good that you may do his will, working in us that which is pleasing in his sight, through Jesus Christ, to whom be glory forever and ever," (13:20-21).

So be it!

*Names changed for security purposes.

[1] Here are other authors who have also done some helpful digging: R. Stanton Norman, ed., *The Mission of Today's Church: Baptist Leaders Look at Modern Faith Issues* (Nashville, TN: B&H Publishing, 2007), 73-94; see Ed Stetzer's chapter, "The Missional Nature of the Church". Zane Pratt, M. David Sills, and Jeff K. Walters, *Introduction to Global Missions* (Nashville, TN: B&H Academic, 2014), 237-252; see Jeff K. Walters' chapter, "The Local Church on Mission". Eckhard J. Schnabel, *Paul the Missionary: Realities, Strategies, and Methods* (Downers Grove, IL: IVP Academic, 2008), 394; see Schabel's footnote with further resources on the church-missions agency relationship.

A Sending

A Sending Church is a local community of Christ-followers who have made a covenant together to be prayerful, deliberate, and proactive in developing, commissioning, and sending their own members both locally and globally, often in partnership with other churches or agencies, and continuing to encourage, support, and advocate for them while making disciples cross-culturally.

What makes you go? Not in the "Go, therefore" or "Daddy, I gotta go!" sense, but just at the most basic level. Go. Move. Do something. Your brain sends signals to your body and it stands. Pretty simple, you know, except for the dozens of muscles and bones it takes working perfectly together, not to mention 60,000 miles of blood vessels escorting millions of cells to the right places just so you can be on your feet.

If that's not mind-blowing enough...what moves the brain in the first place?

Why start a missions article with science? Well, thanks to CBS's *The Big Bang Theory*, geeking is hip. And it reflects perhaps humanity's biggest question: what started all this movement? Some say it was a bang. Others look to an old idea referred to as the cosmological argument. It says basically that nothing moves without first being caused to go. If we traced every movement in the history of the world back, there would have to be something that began the action, a "prime mover." From its first words the Bible points out that this prime mover is God.

In the beginning, God created the heavens and the earth. The earth was without form and void, and darkness was over the face of the deep. And the Spirit of God was hovering over the face of the waters. And God said, "Let there be light," and there was light, Genesis 1:1-3

In the beginning, there's just God. No heavens nor earth. No people. No 'once upon a time'. Only the Triune God being God for eternity past—which honestly makes my brain hurt. We don't know much about what that looked like, but Jesus gives us a hint in his prayer to the Father from John 17:

Father, I want those you have given me to be with me where I am, and to see my glory, the glory you have given me because you loved me before the creation of the world.[1]

The Father, Son, and Spirit expressed glory and love in perfect union. It was an exchange that came straight from the heart of who he is. This is crucial to understanding God not as One who needed to create something, but as One who had it all within himself.[2] From that setting he makes the story as we know it go. How does he do it? The same old expression, this time extended outside himself. He emanates. He initiates. In a sense, he sends. He sends his Spirit to hover over the waters, ready for a word to bring it all to life through the Son. Like so many things in Genesis 1-2, this sets a pattern for how God will keep his story rolling. As a poetic commentary celebrating God's rule over creation, Psalm 104:29-30 describes the crazy way that everything waits on him to move:

When you hide your face, they are dismayed; when you take away their breath, they die and return to their dust. When you send forth your Spirit, they are created, and you renew the face of the earth.

Not simply creating a man and woman, God commissions, or sends, Adam and Eve into the Garden of Eden to "fill the earth and subdue it and have dominion over [it]" (Genesis 1:28). Forget peasants, says T. Desmond Alexander, these guys entered the story as royalty, "God's viceroys [who] govern the earth on his behalf."[3] So it makes sense that the *imago Dei*,[4] the basic way that people mirror God, makes for little sent ones.

And this is not just God's ideal; even after sin corrupts the world he continues to send his Spirit, word, angels, law, messengers, judges, priests, kings, and prophets—not to mention his own Son. Paul writes,

But when the fullness of time had come, God sent forth his Son, born of a woman, born under the law, to redeem those who were under the law, so that we might receive adoption as sons, Galatians 4:5

So it should be no surprise when the Son looks to his own and says, "As the Father has sent me, even so I am sending you" (John 20:21). The information age certainly has its privileges, namely the common knowledge of what many died longing to see—how the missio Dei[5] actually works. The Sender sends the Sent One who sends the Spirit (Acts 13:4) who sends the apostles (note the Greek, *apostolos*, meaning "sent one") who start a chain reaction of sent-ones. The sending only returns to its original form when you track to the end of the story, where you will find not a garden of two, but a city of countless. There the eternal glory and love of the Triune God will no longer be extended outside himself because the people of God will be hidden *in* Christ as "his body, the fullness of him who fills all in all" (Ephesians 1:23). The mission will be complete. New Testament scholar Andreas J. Kostenberger sums it up better than I could:

We have understood the notion of 'mission' as intimately bound up with God's saving plan that moves from creation to new creation, and as framing the entire story of Scripture. It has to do with God's salvation reaching to the ends of the earth: that is, his gracious movement in his Son, the Lord Jesus Christ, to rescue a desperately needy world that is in rebellion against him and stands under his righteous judgment. Clearly the notion of 'sending' is central to any treatment of mission. The Lord of the Scriptures is a missionary God who reaches out to the lost, and sends his servants, and particularly his beloved Son, to achieve his gracious purposes of salvation.[6]

God, out of the overflow of his character, is a Sender. We then, by nature, are sent. The *imago Dei* makes it pulse in our veins. The *missio Dei* moves us to get on our feet and go. So that's why we go. We're sent.

[1] John 17:24, NIV
[2] Michael Reeves, *Delighting in the Trinity: An Introduction to Christian Faith* (Downers Grove, IL: IVP, 2012), 19-20.
[3] T. Desmond Alexander, *From Eden to the New Jerusalem: An Introduction to Biblical Theology* (Grand Rapids, MI: Kregel Academic, 2009), 76.
[4] *Imago Dei* is a Latin phrase that means "image of God"
[5] *Missio Dei* is a Latin phrase that means "mission of God"
[6] Andreas J. Kostenberger, *Salvation to the Ends of the Earth: A Biblical Theology of Mission* (Downers Grove, IL: IVP Academic, 2001), 268-269.

Church

A Sending **Church** is a local community of Christ-followers who have made a covenant together to be prayerful, deliberate, and proactive in developing, commissioning, and sending their own members both locally and globally, often in partnership with other churches or agencies, and continuing to encourage, support, and advocate for them while making disciples cross-culturally.

I didn't even make it to the first security checkpoint before my trip to Israel got *real*. "I came here for vacation?" I thought to myself as teenage women in military fatigues railed me with questions and glares. Finally stumbling off the bus onto the busy streets of Jerusalem, I saw more soldiers on every corner, all of them younger than me. Welcome to the intriguing land of conscription.

An uncommon term in the West, *conscription* is mandatory enlistment in military service. In nations like Israel and many others, conscription seems more of an accepted reality, and maybe even a winch for national pride.[1] This makes service *dutiful*. Americans, however, value voluntary service, wanting to let freedom ring so it remains just that—voluntary. This makes service *optional*.

Often similar sides are taken when it comes to the church and sending. Semantical skirmishes continue to pop up over the topic of who is sent. Just who are the sent ones? Some would say unconditionally that all Christians are missionaries.[2] Others have gone so far as to say that only an elite few are missionaries.[3] Wherever we land in the dialogue, we must beware of blunting God's razor sharp call to mission, a robust biblical theme that's wider than voluntary (Matthew 25:14-30) and deeper than duty (Luke 17:7-9).

All of us marvel over babies having 'their daddy's nose' or 'their mommy's lips'. How much more should it compel our hearts that the *imago Dei* allows humanity to reflect God as Sender! To begin processing the nature of sent ones, first, let's zoom out. Sprawled like a party banner over the entire Bible is the *missio Dei*. In the acclaimed text, *The Mission of God*, Christopher J. H. Wright spends over 500 pages teasing out, not a biblical basis of mission, but a missional basis of the Bible. He writes,

[It's] not just that the Bible contains a number of texts which happen to provide a rationale for missionary endeavor but that the whole Bible is itself a "missional" phenomenon. The writings that now comprise the Bible are themselves the product of and witness to the ultimate mission of God.[4]

This is a bold move, and to some may smack of trickery in the name of scholarship to push a

14

missions agenda. Yet its legitimacy is not so much in the 10 lb. hardback, but the testimony of the eternal Word himself, Jesus Christ. He said that the living word always testifies about him (John 5:39), and that he is always about the Father's mission (John 5:17). The rushing river of *missio Dei* doesn't restrain well into a topical study only when we teach the Book of Acts. It rolls from Eden to New Jerusalem, and we are caught in its currents.

This is where we zoom in. If the *missio Dei* describes broadly what God is about, it also defines narrowly how He gets it done: his little church. The church is the collection of sent ones. One of Mark Dever's helpful nine marks of a healthy church makes clear that the "Bible would seem to indicate that all believers have received this commission."[5] Before we keep calm and carry on, let's play devil's advocate. What if Christians *weren't* so clearly commissioned as "ambassadors for Christ" (2 Corinthians 5:20)? In this, Robert Speer was way ahead of us:

[I]f these particular words had not been spoken by Him...or preserved, the missionary duty of the Church would not be in the least affected. The supreme arguments for missions are not found in any specific words. It is in the very being and character of God.[6]

It really seems impossible to weasel any church out of God's mission. Insert here echoes of old Roland

Allen booming about New Testament churches filled with obedient people who shared the gospel so naturally that Paul didn't need to exhort them to do it in his letters. After all, they had received "the Spirit of Jesus, and the Spirit of Jesus is a missionary spirit".[7] A Spirit who didn't just conscript them to dutiful mission or leave it voluntary for the faithful few.

It was more than activity. It was their identity.

And it's ours too.

[1] The Economist Online. (4 July 2011). *Military Conscription: Does Your Country Need You?* Retrieved from www.economist.com/blogs/dailychart/2011/07/military-conscription.
[2] Robert L. Plummer & John Mark Terry, ed. *Paul's Missionary Methods: In His Time and Ours* (Downers Grove, IL: IVP Academic, 2012), 91; see Christoph Stenschke where he argues that lines were blurred between congregation and missionary in the New Testament.
[3] Cross Conference. (2014) *Panel with John Piper and Mark Dever.* Retrieved from crosscon.com/media/2013/12/cross-2013-panel-with-john-piper-and-mark-dever/. Here John Piper distinguishes between narrowly-defined types of missionaries.
[4] Christopher J. H. Wright, *The Mission of God: Unlocking the Bible's Grand Narrative* (Downers Grove, IL: IVP Academic, 2013), 22.
[5] Mark Dever, *Nine Marks of a Healthy Church* (Wheaton, IL: Crossway, 2013), 124.
[6] George W. Peters, *A Biblical Theology of Missions* (Chicago, IL: Moody, 1984), 55; here Peters quotes Robert Speer.
[7] Roland Allen, *Missionary Methods: St. Paul's or Ours?* (Seattle: CreateSpace, 2012), 93.

is a

> A Sending Church **is a** local community of Christ-
> followers who have made a covenant together to be
> prayerful, deliberate, and proactive in developing,
> commissioning, and sending their own members
> both locally and globally, often in partnership with
> other churches or agencies, and continuing to
> encourage, support, and advocate for them while
> making disciples cross-culturally.

We all love the power of one. The rags to riches
story of the underdog who pulls himself up by his
bootstraps and arrives as the self-made CEO of his
universe. By the story's end, all he needs is a bigger
backpack—'cause he's carrying everybody. Subtle
case in point: the 2014 NFL Pro Bowl, which
confusingly was no longer promoted simply as one
region's best players versus the other's, but was all
of sudden "Team Rice vs. Team Sanders," based on
the alumni team captains, Hall of Famers Jerry Rice
and Deion Sanders.[1] Hat tip to the NFL's marketing
attempt—they know we dig the power of one. It's a
picture of our innate longing for Jesus, the One with
"the sins of the earth strapped on his back." [2]

Yet the manifest destiny that sparks in each of us
mellows in most of us by our thirties. I realized I
would never be the next Michael Jordan in high
school, and so began the process of settling for less.
Our dreams live on in those who do what we

17

couldn't. The power of one is surrendered to the heroes of our culture, while we snuggle into our beanbag chairs and watch them.

The discussion of the Sending Church may leave some individuals and churches feeling left in a beanbag chair. The definition seems big and daunting. Many of the churches touted as sending churches are big and daunting. Why not leave it up to the so-called experts, the big churches and missions agencies? Great question. Let's pull our beanbag chairs together and talk.

Discussions about the church and mission are often rooted in great biblical examples. But instead of garnering the power of a church from Team Jerusalem and Team Antioch, let's start with the benchwarmers. Jesus makes it clear that his motley crew of disciples stood upon "the foundation of the church"[3]:

And I tell you, you are Peter, and on this rock I will build my church, and the gates of hell shall not prevail against it, Matthew 16:18

Of course, we understand this "rock" rightly in context as Peter's confession, "You are the Christ, the Son of the living God" (v. 16). A couple of things make these words absolutely remarkable. First, they are sandwiched between two episodes of Homer Simpson "D'oh!" moments for the disciples.

In verses 5-12 Jesus was baffled that they were still stuck on bread after seeing the Bread of Life miraculously feed thousands—*twice*. In verses 21-23 Jesus was fuming as Peter unknowingly teamed with Satan to keep the suffering servant from going to the cross. Yet, as Kevin DeYoung and Greg Gilbert remind us, it is to "this ragtag bunch of argumentative, self-centered, struggling-for-holiness but gloriously forgiven sinners—that the keys of the kingdom of God are given."[4] The invitation to mission for every church doesn't begin with who they could be, but who they are: broken, but God's.

Second, Jesus' words give a ridiculous promise to the church, the world's greatest underdog: "I will build my church, and the gates of hell shall not prevail against it." It's like the secret of our greatest sports heroes. Babe Ruth was crazy enough to step up to the plate in the World Series and point to the center field bleachers because he was actually convinced he could hit a home run on demand. How much more bold, then, can a church be when the mission is guaranteed! As Keith Whitfield puts it, "If the church shapes and orients its mission around God's mission, it will not fail."[5] Christopher Wright adds,

We are seeking to accomplish what God himself wills to happen. This is both humbling and reassuring...For we know that behind all our fumbling efforts...stands the supreme will of the living God.[6]

Every church can step up to the plate and point toward center because Jesus *will* accomplish his mission. But this doesn't mean they must have all-stars at every position. Tom Telford has contributed an encouraging voice in this regard with his book, *Today's All-Star Missions Churches.* He calls churches out of the stands and onto the field:

[Many] churches have found their particular skill in missions and are throwing their strength into doing that one thing well. We all can't do everything. Some churches don't have the manpower, staff, or financial resources to do what others can do. Thinking, however, that if they can't do it all, they won't do anything is not a good mindset for churches.[7]

Every church has something to offer. Yes, every church's contribution is just a drop in the bucket. But what a bucket! And what a leader who, by the way he addresses churches in Revelation 2-3, wants every drop that is due him. The Sending Church discussion is for a church, every church.

¹ Kevin Patra. (26 January 2014). *Team Rice Defeats Team Sanders in NFL Pro Bowl*. Retrieved from www.nfl.com/news/story/0ap2000000318206/article/team-rice-defeats-team-sanders-in-nfl-pro-bowl.

² Sojourn Music (20 November 2012). *The Day the Sky Went Black*. Retrieved from https://sojournmusic.bandcamp.com/track/the-day-the-sky-went-black.

³ Gregg R. Allison, *Sojourners and Strangers: The Doctrine of the Church* (Wheaton, IL: Crossway, 2012).

⁴ Kevin DeYoung and Greg Gilbert, *What is the Mission of the Church? Making Sense of Shalom, Social Justice, and the Great Commission* (Wheaton, IL: Crossway, 2011), 126-127.

⁵ Bruce Riley Ashford, ed. *Theology and Practice of Mission: God, the Church, and the Nations* (Nashville, TN: B&H Academic, 2011), 17; see Keith Whitfield's chapter, "The Triune God: The God of Mission".

⁶ Christopher J. H. Wright, *The Mission of God: Unlocking the Bible's Grand Narrative* (Downers Grove, IL: IVP Academic, 2013), 129.

⁷ Tom Telford, *Today's All-Star Missions Churches: Strategies to Help Your Church Get Into the Game* (Grand Rapids, MI: Baker Books, 2001), 149.

local

A Sending Church is a **local** community of Christ-followers who have made a covenant together to be prayerful, deliberate, and proactive in developing, commissioning, and sending their own members both locally and globally, often in partnership with other churches or agencies, and continuing to encourage, support, and advocate for them while making disciples cross-culturally.

An Evangelical squabble commenced in early 2014 when story aficionado Donald Miller blogged a confession about why he doesn't go to church very often, describing church services as personally insufficient for connecting him with God.[1] Tweets were flying like the simultaneous strange snowfall in Atlanta and people were gridlocked for hours not only on the interstate, but the topic of the local church. Several church leaders like Mike Cosper publicly rebutted Miller as prophetic about the lack of spiritual formation in many churches, but ultimately contributing to the dilemma and its affects —namely, a culture of bailing on the church.[2] Miller was certainly not the first proponent of you-love-her-when-you-let-her-go ecclesiology (as he mentioned in his response to the mad tweeters[3]), nor the first to go public. George Barna offered a similar notion in his book *Revolution: Finding Vibrant Faith Beyond the Walls of the Sanctuary*:

Scripture teaches us that devoting your life to loving God with all your heart, mind, strength, and soul is what honors Him. Being part of a local church may facilitate that. Or it might not...millions of believers have moved beyond the established church.[4]

"Notice all of the emphasis on what the individuals do," theologian Michael Horton responded to Barna.[5] Look a little closer and you'll see the Trojan horse used to siege the local church: Both Miller and Barna leveraged identity as the *universal* church to justify opting out of the *local* church. "It's almost as though [Jesus] sees the church as one, without walls, denominations or tribes," said Miller. Indeed, Jesus uses both "eyes of flaming fire" (Revelation 1:14) to see with perfect clarity his church as both universal and local.[6] Wear an eye patch if you like—Jesus doesn't.

Yet Western individualistic culture may not be the only one leaving the local church out of the game. For years some missions organizations have shepherded the universal church in ways that exclude local churches' direct involvement in mission, let alone their leadership in it. Whether spoken or not, their cry has been, *We do mission **on behalf** of local churches.* Granted, this was not necessarily manipulative—it was passionate. Nor was it one-sided—many churches farmed it out gladly to the "professionals". The missions agency has contributed much and continues to have a valuable role in mission. Theologian, missionary, pastor, and professor Eric Wright describes this role as a *partner*:

Without vibrant sending churches, the whole missionary enterprise falters. The local church is the nursery where missionary vision is nurtured, the base from which missionaries are sent and the home to which they return for encouragement and rest. Local churches and mission boards are partners in the great missionary task.[7]

But this is not a partnership between equals. Traditionally, churches have been the water boys cheering on missions organizations as they take the field. The concept of sending church calls for a permanent substitution. Rather than a novel innovation of forward-thinking church leaders, the *missio Dei* as defined by the Scriptures has always beckoned for the local church's leading role. Jedidiah Coppenger describes it this way:

Any articulation of the missio Dei that fails to include the [church] fails to understand the mission... Christ is creating more and more kingdom outposts; he is creating local churches...the proclamation of the gospel of the kingdom creates and sounds forth from the church.[8]

Does this mean that missions organizations should cease? Until the day of Christ, may it never be! It does, however, call for a renewed posture, one that gasps at the beautiful bride of Christ "which he obtained with his own blood" (Acts 20:28), one that cheers her to mission rather than usurping her role. Sending churches are eager to partner, but desire more than a place at the table of experts. They are the local expressions of the body of Christ who are living out the mandate "to not only address [their] own needs and matters, but also to partake in God's vision and mission for this world".[9] They are the ones for whom Jesus substituted himself that they might take the field through the Holy Spirit. They are the ones through whom the "manifold wisdom of God might now be made known" (Ephesians 3:10). They are the ones among whom Jesus walks as lamp stands through which he shines into the world (Revelation 1:12, 20).

So in Jesus' own words, "he who has an ear, let him hear what the Spirit says to the churches."

1 Donald Miller. (3 February 2014). *I Don't Worship God By Singing. I Connect With Him* Elsewhere. Retrieved from http://storylineblog.com/2014/02/03/i-dont-worship-god-by-singing-i-connect-with-him-elsewhere/.
2 Mike Cosper. (5 February 2014). *Donald Miller and the Culture of Contemporary* Worship. Retrieved from http://www.mikedcosper.com/home/donald-miller-and-the-culture-of-contemporary-worship.
3 Donald Miller. (5 February 2014). *Why I Don't Go to Church Very Often, A Follow* Up. Retrieved from http://storylineblog.com/2014/02/05/why-i-dont-go-to-church-very-often-a-follow-up-blog/.
4 George Barna, *Revolution: Finding Vibrant Faith Beyond the Walls of the Sanctuary* (Carol Stream, IL: Tyndale Momentum, 2012).
5 Michael S. Horton, *People and Place: A Covenant Ecclesiology* (Louisville, KY: Westminster John Knox, 2008), 177.
6 John Frame, *Systematic Theology: An Introduction to Christian Belief* (Philipsburg, NJ: P&R Publishing, 2013), 1020.
7 Eric E. Wright, *A Practical Theology of Missions: Dispelling the Mystery; Recovering the Passion* (Leominster, UK: Day One Publications, 2010), 227.
8 Bruce Riley Ashford, ed. *Theology and Practice of Mission: God, the Church, and the Nations* (Nashville, TN: B&H Academic, 2011), 74-75; see Jedediah Coppenger's chapter, "The Community of Mission: The Church".
9 Robert L. Plummer & John Mark Terry, ed. *Pau's Missionary Methods: In His Time and Ours* (Downers Grove, IL: IVP Academic, 2012), 94; see Christoph Stenschke's chapter, "Paul's Mission as the Mission of the Church".

community

A Sending Church is a local **community** of Christ-followers who have made a covenant together to be prayerful, deliberate, and proactive in developing, commissioning, and sending their own members both locally and globally, often in partnership with other churches or agencies, and continuing to encourage, support, and advocate for them while making disciples cross-culturally.

The compelling miniseries *Band of Brothers* captured a new generation with its modern depiction of renowned US Army paratroopers of the 121st Airborne's Easy Company during World War II. Their gut-wrenching story is traced from the beginning to the end of the war, and is summed up well in this famous quote from one of the episodes:

Men, it's been a long war, it's been a tough war. You've fought bravely, proudly for your country. You're a special group. You've found in one another a bond that exists only in combat, among brothers. You've shared foxholes, held each other in dire moments. You've seen death and suffered together. I'm proud to have served with each and every one of you. You all deserve long and happy lives in peace.[1]

It's often been said that in the throes of war soldiers fight not so much for the cause, but for one another. Though typically complete strangers, the sense of brotherhood that develops among them from striving, suffering, and dying together lasts a lifetime. It may be the most awe-inspiring picture of community the world has to offer.

Yet it still falls far short of the kind of community Jesus gives to his church on mission.

The term community has been growing in popularity since the chat-room days of the Internet. Yet its roots are traceable a bit further—try eternity past. The original community, the richest and purest and most admirable and missional, is found in the Triune God. Jedidiah Coppenger says,

God's mission has eternally had a community of mission, Father, Son, and Spirit. God's trinitarian nature not only shows us the necessity of community for God's mission; it also shows us the goal of God's mission, which is his glory.[2]

So we might say that community begins in Genesis 1:1 with the one true God.[3] And as the *missio Dei* is fleshed out in the rest of the Bible, "God-the-community creates a community to join him in his community mission for his glory."[4] The body of Christ reflects and glorifies its Head brilliantly in community, particularly as it strives (to know him), suffers (his sufferings), and dies *together* (to sin, the flesh, the world—and sometimes literally—Philippians 3:10-11). In *Paul the Missionary*, Eckhard Schnabel describes the two-fold purpose of the church's gathering as being edified by the written Word and meeting with the living Word.[5] It is this Word who seeks "that [the church] may all be one...so that the world may believe that you have sent me" (John 17:21).

But this measure of heavenly community is only possible in the trenches. Soldiers go home seeking long and happy lives in peace. In this world, however, there is no such thing for the church. Since I couldn't just write, 'Read Bonhoeffer,' we do well here to quote him at length:

It is not simply to be taken for granted that the Christian has the privilege of living among other Christians. Jesus Christ lived in the midst of his enemies...For this cause he had come, to bring peace to the enemies of God. So the Christian, too, belongs not in the seclusion of a cloistered life but in the thick of foes. There is his commission, his work. 'The kingdom is to be in the midst of your enemies. And he who will not suffer this does not want to be of the Kingdom of Christ; he wants to be among friends, to sit among roses and lilies, not with the bad people but the devout people. O you blasphemers and betrayers of Christ! If Christ had done what you are doing who would ever have been spared?'"[6]

Make no mistake, "there is church because there is mission, not vice versa."[7] Community that isn't on mission isn't community. That statement will get pushback, however, because it has throughout church history. According to Daniel Montgomery, Eastern churches have historically focused on community (think monasticism), while Western churches have drilled mission (think tent revivals).[8] Why are community and mission the antithesis of one another in the church? European church leaders Tim Chester and Steve Timmis say it doesn't have to be this way. From the trenches of secularization they have written *Everyday Church: Gospel Communities on Mission*, using 1 Peter to describe how the church is meant to thrive in the margins of society as they live communally on mission in everyday life. "This is how God defines the good life: the people of God together in community making known the glory of God. This is the gospel."[9]

Consider it, a gospel where not only wrath *and* mercy meet, but community *and* mission. Sending churches find the bliss of communion in the shrapnel of mission.

¹ *Band of Brothers*, "Points". Directed by Mikael Salomon. USA: DreamWorks, 2001.

² Bruce Riley Ashford, ed. *Theology and Practice of Mission: God, the Church, and the Nations* (Nashville, TN: B&H Academic, 2011), 75; see Jedediah Coppenger's chapter, "The Community of Mission: The Church".

³ R. Albert Mohler, Jr. (13 February 2014). *Monotheism is Not Enough*. Retrieved from http://www.sbts.edu/resources/chapel/monotheism-is-not-enough/.

⁴ Ashford, *Mission*, 75.

⁵ Eckhard J. Schnabel, *Paul the Missionary: Realities, Strategies, and Methods* (Downers Grove, IL: IVP Academic, 2008), 422.

⁶ Dietrich Bonhoeffer, *Life Together* (New York, NY: HarperOne, 2009),18; the quotation within the quote is from Martin Luther.

⁷ David J. Bosch, *Transforming Mission: Paradigm Shifts in Theology of Mission* (Maryknoll, NY: Orbis Books, 2011, 390.

⁸ Daniel Montgomery. (19 January 2014). *State of Communion*. Retrieved from http://sojournchurch.com/sermons/state-of-communion/.

⁹ Tim Chester and Steve Timmis, *Everyday Church: Gospel Communities on Mission* (Wheaton, IL: Crossway, 2012), 160.

# of Christ-followers

A Sending Church is a local community **of Christ-followers** who have made a covenant together to be prayerful, deliberate, and proactive in developing, commissioning, and sending their own members both locally and globally, often in partnership with other churches or agencies, and continuing to encourage, support, and advocate for them while making disciples cross-culturally.

If we breezed through all the previous topics and thought, 'Yeah, we can do this,' then the time has come for us to drop our devices and bury our faces in our hands. Jesus said, "If anyone would come after me, let him deny himself and take up his cross and follow me" (Matthew 16:24). The implications are nothing less than death. One thinks straightway of Dietrich Bonhoeffer's famous quote from *The Cost of Discipleship*, "When Christ calls a man, he bids him come and die."[1] David Platt continues this theme in *Follow Me*, describing the one who calls:

We are overwhelmed by the magnitude of the words "follow me" because we are awed by the majesty of the "me" who says them...Jesus is not some puny religious teacher begging for an invitation from anyone. He is the all-sovereign Lord who deserves submission from everyone.[2]

Who is fit to follow such a one? Joseph Hart's 18th century hymn reminds us:

Let not conscience make you linger,
Not of fitness fondly dream;
All the fitness He requireth
Is to feel your need of Him.[3]

Amazingly, by God's grace, words, and Spirit, people are able to feel their need, hear their shepherd's voice, and follow him. This is and always has been the greatest miracle in the world.

Then all true Christ-followers, some sooner than others, begin to realize more fully the dying they've been made alive to. As Nik Ripken heralds on behalf of Somali Christians, we are meant to wince when we take the Lord's Supper.[4] God spared himself no expense in our salvation, and he spares us no expense in our sanctification. Here, it's helpful to use "Christ-followers" in place of "church" because it reminds us that "[we] are not [our] own, for [we] were bought with a price" (1 Corinthians 6:19). The surgery we undergo as the Spirit removes our every cancerous nodule of self-dependence is actually what we signed up for when we followed the one who "although he was a son, learned obedience through what he suffered" (Hebrews 5:8).

What does this have to do with the sending church? It's the necessary setup for remembering that the mission itself isn't our own either. The *"Lord* of the harvest" directs us to pray earnestly to him for *"his* harvest" (Luke 10:2, emphasis mine). And he corrects us when we're distracted by our own missions (Luke 10:17-20). Were we given the freedom to choose the mission, we would most certainly go for something less risky,[5] less bloody,[6] less insane.[7] And isn't that often what we've done? Without sending, our churches look more like Babel than Antioch. Instead, our steepled towers are meant to be distribution centers

not measured by church attendance or activities...
With hearts set on Jesus, the author and finisher of
their faith, [Christ-followers] gladly submit to the
responsibility given to his church. Willing to go
anywhere—longing for the message of hope to go
everywhere—they hear the voice of the Shepherd
and follow him![8]

But "how are they to preach unless they are sent?" Romans 10:15 asks poignantly. Outside our beloved elites who sense a missionary call and pursue it, most Christ-followers have no idea of their sent-ness. Bruce Ware's *Father, Son, and Holy Spirit* would be a huge encouragement to them in describing the Son and Spirit's willing eternal posture toward the Father's sending as evidence of every Christian's sent nature—but it's probably not on their coffee table.[9] Yet neither was he on the Moravians' coffee tables, and they became arguably the greatest sending church the world has seen thus far. How'd they do it? Through the

emphasis that every Christian is a missionary and should witness through his daily vocation. If the example of the Moravians had been studied more carefully by other Christians, it is possible that the businessman might have retained his honored place within the expanding Christian world mission, beside the preacher, teacher, and physician.[10]

So becoming a sending church seems to begin with helping every member understand they are sent, then moves toward equipping them to live that way.[11] At its easiest point that means sending everyone. Teens. Housewives. Execs. But at its hardest point that also means sending everyone— because you'll lose great leaders to start new churches, to burn out, to go overseas, to be killed[12]— to follow Christ. Roland Allen called this "generational resubmission," the need for each generation of the church to resubmit their "traditions of men to the Word and the Spirit of God."[13] Larry McCrary simply called it, "following the Spirit," the utmost missionary tradecraft.[14]

Jesus just says, "Follow me."

1 Dietrich Bonhoeffer, *The Cost of Discipleship* (New York, NY: Simon and Schuster, 1959), 99.

2 David Platt, *Follow Me: A Call to Die, A Call to Live* (Carol Stream, IL: Tyndale House Publishers, 2013), 38.

3 Sojourn Music (20 November 2012). *Come Ye Sinners.* Retrieved from http://sojournmusic.bandcamp.com/track/come-ye-sinners.

4 Nik Ripken. (20 October 2013). *A Present Tense Resurrection.* Retrieved from http://east.sojournchurch.com/sermons/a-present-tense-resurrection-nik-ripken/.

5 John Piper. (4 January 2007). *The Power to Risk in the Cause of Christ.* Retrieved from http://www.desiringgod.org/conference-messages/the-power-to-risk-in-the-cause-of-christ.

6 Zach Bradley. (16 December 2013). *Blood on Both Ends of the Rope: A Broader Definition of the Sending Church.* Retrieved from http://international.sojournchurch.com/?p=4416.

7 Nik Ripken, *The Insanity of God: A True Story of Faith Resurrected* (Nashville, TN: B&H Books, 2013).

8 Mike Barnett, ed. *Discovering the Mission of God: Best Missional Practices for the 21st Century* (Downers Grove, IL: IVP Academic, 2012), 601; see H. Al Gilbert's chapter, "The Local Church and the Mission of God".

9 Bruce A. Ware, *Father, Son, and Holy Spirit: Relationships, Roles, and Relevance* (Wheaton, IL: Crossway, 2005).

10 Ruth A Tucker, *From Jerusalem to Irian Jaya: A Biographical History of Christian Missions* (Grand Rapids, MI: Zondervan, 2004), 99; quote is taken from William Danker.

11 Jason C. Dukes, *Live Sent: You Are A Letter* (Birmingham, AL: New Hope Publishers, 2011).

12 CBS News. (19 December 2013). *Widow of American Teacher Shot in Libya Says She Forgives Husband's Attackers.* Retrieved from http://www.cbsnews.com/news/widow-of-american-teacher-shot-in-libya-says-she-forgives-husbands-attackers/.

13 Robert L Plummer and John Mark Terry, *Paul's Missionary Methods: In His Time and Ours* (Downers Grove, IL: IVP Academic, 2012), 127; quote is taken from Roland Allen.

14 Larry McCrary, Caleb Crider, Wade Stephens and Rodney Calfee, *Tradecraft: For the Church on Mission* (Portland, OR: Urban Loft Publishers, 2013), 34-49.

who have made a covenant

A Sending Church is a local community of Christ-followers **who have made a covenant** together to be prayerful, deliberate, and proactive in developing, commissioning, and sending their own members both locally and globally, often in partnership with other churches or agencies, and continuing to encourage, support, and advocate for them while making disciples cross-culturally.

A sending church is *all in*. A culture of sending only comes out of a culture of being all in. And being all in means covenant.

Covenant is an idea we have to blow the dust off of in our culture. Marriage used to be our teacher, but with the shifting attitude toward covenant relationship in America, it looks like even the church needs a substitute on the subject.[1] Thankfully, one is available—and he wrote the definition. God expresses himself quite naturally through covenant. Gregg Allison says that "from the created order to human beings, every relationship in which God has been engaged has been structured according to some type of covenant."[2] Ever wondered what it's like to be God? Well, for one, when your presence alone makes others' faces melt like in *Indiana Jones and the Raiders of the Lost Ark*, your relationships must come with certain terms and boundaries.

37

Today we live in the crazy era of God's last and greatest covenant. The whole game changed when Jesus became "the mediator of a new covenant, so that those who are called may receive the promised eternal inheritance" (Hebrews 9:15). These terms of agreement come not with allegiance to a law, but surrender to a Person, as Spurgeon put it,

Come and try him. I do not ask thee to lay hold on the whole covenant, thou shalt do that by-and-by; but lay hold on Christ, and if thou wilt do that, then thou hast the covenant.[3]

But how is it determined who has evidently entered this covenant; entered into Christ? This responsibility God has been given to Christ's body, the church. After Jesus proclaimed that he would build his church on the rock of confession that he is the Christ, he said to Peter and the apostles, "I will give you the keys of the kingdom of heaven, and whatever you bind on earth shall be bound in heaven, and whatever you loose on earth shall be loosed in heaven" (Matthew 16:19). Here, the apostles as leaders-to-be of the church were given the authority to discern who God says are his. For Evangelicals this might feel very Catholic. For the world, this probably feels egomaniacal and exclusive. Hopefully for churches, it feels like a necessary and weighty privilege.

And this is where things get squirrely. Jonathan Leeman, in his helpful little book, Church

Membership, says that most people look at church as either a club or a service provider.[4] Secularism has breached church levees more than we'd like to admit, and Jesus' authoritative "embassy" on earth is often ruled instead by pretty much *whatever people want*. A relationship based solely on services provided has historically been called prostitution. Today, relationship without covenant is the new normal, but it still prostitutes. Consumer church is no different.

So, the covenant God has a covenant family. If pastors are "to care for the church of God, which he obtained with his own blood" (Acts 20:28) "as those who will have to give an account" (Hebrews 13:17), they must know which sheep to shepherd. If believers are "individually members of one another" (Romans 12:5), they must know to whom they belong. "Christians don't join churches," says Leeman, "they submit to them."[5] Daniel Montgomery and Mike Cosper add:

This commitment is mutual. By committing myself to the church, I'm committed to a body of people who is, in turn, committed to me...it's a promise to look out for one another, a way of saying, "I'm in, I'm about this, and I want us to mutually journey together toward Jesus."[6]

This sort of commitment also includes a confession: *we need each other*. If Matthew 16 established the church's authority to affirm who enters the flock,

Matthew 18 gives the authority to decide who must leave it. After pointing out the process for correcting a believer who refuses to repent, Jesus says to "let him be to you as a Gentile and a tax collector. Truly, I say to you, whatever you bind on earth shall be bound in heaven, and whatever you loose on earth shall be loosed in heaven (vv. 17-18).

We need each other because we all have "evil and unbelieving thoughts and desires that lead us to fall away from our living God."[7] The covenant God binds us to himself and his covenant family. He knows and keeps watch over his own so he can send them (Mark 3:14). So, ironically, it's the church who knows and keeps watch over its own who is well on its way toward sending them.

[1] Robert P. Jones, Daniel Cox, and Juhem Navarro-Rivera. (26 February 2014). *A Shifting Landscape.* Retrieved from http://publicreligion.org/site/wp-content/uploads/2014/02/2014.LGBT_REPORT.pdf?utm_source=Albert+Mohler&utm_campaign=c7b98e7d9c-The_Briefing_2013&utm_medium=email&utm_term=0_b041ba0d12-c7b98e7d9c-307182206.
[2] Gregg R. Allison, *Sojourners and Strangers: The Doctrine of the Church* (Wheaton, IL: Crossway, 2012), 64.
[3] C. H. Spurgeon. (31 August 1856). *Christ in the Covenant.* Retrieved from http://www.spurgeon.org/sermons/0103.htm.
[4] Jonathan Leeman, *Church Membership: How the World Knows Who Represents Jesus* (Wheaton, IL: Crossway, 2012), 65.
[5] Ibid., 91.
[6] Daniel Montgomery and Mike Cosper, *Faithmapping: A Gospel Atlas for Your Spiritual Journey* (Wheaton, IL: Crossway, 2013), 135.
[7] Robert K. Cheong, *God Redeeming His Bride: A Handbook for Church Discipline* (Scotland, UK: Christian Focus Publiscations, 2013), 10.

together

A Sending Church is a local community of Christ-followers who have made a covenant **together** to be prayerful, deliberate, and proactive in developing, commissioning, and sending their own members both locally and globally, often in partnership with other churches or agencies, and continuing to encourage, support, and advocate for them while making disciples cross-culturally.

The Cause

Superglue is pretty amazing stuff. Invented by accident, the powerful glop is now a bestie to surgeons, carpenters, and engineers. But you can also do some damage with it. In grade school a particularly devious classmate came up with the idea of dabbing a little superglue on someone's head behind their ear, then pressing their ear against it. At first it was funny, then painful, then horrifying. The point of the story: superglue binds things together.

Covenant, however, performs a far greater act of binding. It's woven throughout the sending church concepts, and we'll point back to it over and over. But it's not the superglue. Colossians 1:17 makes it clear what is: "[Christ] is before all things, and in him all things hold together." The New Testament consistently pounds not new initiative, but new identity, as Brad House describes, "It is not that Paul wants the church to do more. He wants them to be more."[1]

Covenant is more than binding ourselves to ideals or lists, it's a reminder of whose we are. And whose we are implies whose mission we're a part of. Dietrich Bonhoeffer made the connection insightfully:

[The church] is the salt of the earth. They are the earth's most noble possession, its most precious asset...As those bound only to Jesus, they are directed to the earth, whose salt they are...It is not for the disciples to decide whether they are or are not to be the salt...Those who have been called by Jesus and stand in his discipleship are, through precisely that call, the salt of the earth in their entire existence.[2]

The church, bound to and held together by Christ, is given (or sent) to the earth. Covenanting together is the intentional, ongoing recognition of that.

This is spelled out beautifully as Jesus' desire for his church is laid bare in John 17. What's the big idea? Glory—Jesus is consumed with the Father's glory. He wants the Father to be glorified through his sacrifice and the gathering together of his church. But that's not all. Jesus sums up the major themes of his prayer near the end: "The glory that you have given me I have given to them, that they may be one even as we are one...so that the world may know that you sent me" (vv. 22-23). Glory, unity, mission. Jim Belcher applies it this way:

For the deep church, the gospel is at the center...As we are affected by the gospel, we are empowered to move into community to care for one another. And as we care for one another, we begin to reach outside of our community with...mission.[3]

Being all in together also helps avoid mission misfires. *What is the Mission of the Church?* goes to great lengths in *kindly* narrowing the definition: "mission is not everything the church does, but rather describes 'everything the church is sent into the world to do.'"[4] Covenant helps keep the main thing the main thing. It also keeps mission from being an individual whim or burden. Gregg Allison deserves the mic here:

being missional is a matter of corporate identity first, then individual engagement...'If, for evangelicalism, Christian faith and identity are first personal and individual, its sense of missions tends to be the same. The responsibility to give witness to Christ is one each person bears. The accent rests on personal evangelism...thus, 'missions in the end does not belong to the church.'"[5]

Probably an entire book could be given to this issue. As churches have outsourced mission, they have effectively individualized it. Thus, being a sent one is a personal preference rather than part of a corporate identity. And being sent globally has been left to those, well, with the gumption to do it. This explains why missionary wannabes tend to approach church leaders with a personal calling and plan already in place—*just sign my church affirmation form and I'll be on my way,* they say. Yet covenant calls them to not only ask what Christ's church can do for them, but what they can do for Christ's church.

According to The Gospel Coalition, calling people to a high bar of covenant membership goes hand in hand with mission.[6] "Raising the spiritual temperature" naturally sweats out those who aren't about Christ and his mission, yet at the same time draws outsiders to the spectacle of missional community. But the bar is for church leaders too. Knowing and keeping their own may lead them to hold tightly and send sparingly. They may be tempted to send the misfits rather than the best.[7] Covenanting together reminds them that they too are bound to the Sender and his mission.

The Effect

My wife and I always argue over the movie *Titanic.* It comes up in conversation, she comments how sweet it was, and then I open my mouth. I'm convinced it wasn't all that sweet. Even if you haven't seen the famous film, you would know by the sheer presence of Leonardo DiCaprio that there's going to be a tragic ending. The romance of Jack and Rose builds and builds, then it happens—she lets go. Not figuratively. She literally lets him float away stiffer than the board she's floating on. Yeah, real sweet.

Thankfully, there's no floating away when it comes to the sending church. As Sojourn Community Church missions pastor, Nathan Garth, often says, "We want to send and never let go."[8] The kind of intentional binding that's reflected in William Carey's famous statement, "I will go down, if you will hold the rope,"[9] leads to burns on everyone's hands—because the entire church is laying hold of the mission together. But more than just a call to action, covenant is a reminder of who the church is, as Tim Chester and Steve Timmis put it:

By becoming a Christian, I belong to God and I belong to my brothers and sisters. It is not that I belong to God and then make a decision to join a local church. My being in Christ means being in Christ with those others who are in Christ. This is my identity. This is our identity... If the church is the body of Christ, then we should not live as disembodied Christians.[10]

If those on earth who don't know Christ are like zombies, the walking dead, then those on mission apart from church are like ghosts, the disembodied living. As Paul puts it, the privilege of the member is

45

being part of the whole body, Christ's very own body (1 Corinthians 12:12-31). That has massive implications for mission. In *Missional God, Missional Church*, scholar and pastor Ross Hastings squeezes 333 pages of Trinitarian communal mission from the sponge of John 20:19-23, stressing that "the church as one with Christ (not individuals) is God's primary missionary."[11] Take *that* in. Together, the church is God's missionary to the world. It's not just that it *produces* individual missionaries. It *is* the missionary.

So we would be right to deduce that there are endless benefits to being on mission together. 3 John 6-8 unpacks the heart of it as John commends and encourages the church's care for sent ones:

You do well to send them on their journey in a manner worthy of God. For they have gone out for the sake of the name, accepting nothing from the Gentiles. Therefore we ought to support people like these, that we may be fellow workers for the truth.

Christopher J. H. Wright points to the worshipful nature of the church sending together.[12] What honor we bestow on God when we send missionaries in the same way we would send Jesus himself! How sweet to be sent out provisioned and prayed for and cried over! And what awe and wonder fuels the body of Christ when everyone recognizes they are co-workers for the truth!

But wait, there's more. Jesus' sending of seventy-two followers in Luke 10 showcases other important effects. There we see training in community (9:1-6), sending *in* community (v. 1), sending *to* community (v. 7), and returning to community (v. 17). The disciples benefited from the entire group as they were developed, which according to Ephesians 4:11-16 is necessary for the building up of the body of Christ. They were sent two by two, never alone, which is the flavor Paul always preferred (see Acts 17:15). They were sent to find households that would welcome their message of peace as little kingdom outposts, which would be groups that spread the word together. They then came back to debrief with one another, being mutually encouraged and sharpened by their Savior and his gospel (v. 20).

Imagine these movements in the church today.

Now imagine the contrast. Training alone. Sending alone. Serving alone. Returning alone. It's ghostly. Not everyone can be a Bruce Olson, who braved the unengaged jungles of Columbia completely by himself.[13] Really, no one should ever be.

Unlike *Titanic*, God's romancing of his church builds and builds, but it doesn't disappoint. He is one who never lets go (Joshua 1:5, Psalm 139:10, Matthew 28:20), and his sending church does the same.

47

[1] Brad House, *Community: Taking Your Small Group Off Life Support* (Wheaton, IL: Crossway, 2011), 17.
[2] Dietrich Bonhoeffer, *Meditations on the Cross* (Louisville, KY: Westminster John Knox Press, 1998), 80-81.
[3] Jim Belcher, *Deep Church: A Third Way Beyond Emerging and Traditional* (Downers Grove, IL: IVP Books, 2009), 121.
[4] Kevin DeYoung and Greg Gilbert, *What is the Mission of the Church? Making Sense of Social Justice, Shalom, and the Great Commission* (Wheaton, IL: Crossway, 2011), 20; the quotation within the quote is from John Stott.
[5] Gregg R. Allison, *Sojourners and Strangers: The Doctrine of the Church* (Wheaton, IL: Crossway, 2012), 147.
[6] Matt Chandler, Mike McKinley, and Jonathan Leeman. (2013). *Membership and Mission: Why Membership Matters for the Church's Mission.* Retrieved from http://resources.thegospelcoalition.org/library/membership-and-mission-why-membership-matters-for-the-church-s-mission-9marks-panel-discussion-mike-mckinley-jonathan-leeman.
[7] David Horner, *When Missions Shapes the Mission: You and Your Church Can Reach the World* (Nashville, TN: B&H Books, 2011).
[8] Nathan Garth. *Sojourn International Mission Convictions.* Retrieved from http://theupstreamcollective.org/wp-content/uploads/2011/11/MISSION-CONVICTIONS-Sojourn-.pdf.
[9] John Piper, *Andrew Fuller: I Will Go Down If You Will Hold the Rope!* (Minneapolis, MN: Desiring God, 2012).
[10] Tim Chester and Steve Timmis, *Total Church: A Radical Reshaping Around Gospel and Community* (Wheaton, IL: Crossway, 2008), 41.
[11] Ross Hastings, *Missional God, Missional Church: Hope for Re-Evangelizing the West* (Downers Grove, IL: IVP Academic, 2012), 128.
[12] Christopher J. H. Wright, *The Mission of God's People: A Biblical Theology of the Church's Mission* (Grand Rapids, MI: Zondervan, 2010), 219.
[13] Bruce Olson, *Bruchko* (Lake Mary, FL: Charisma House, 1977).

to be

> A Sending Church is a local community of Christ-followers who have made a covenant together **to be** prayerful, deliberate, and proactive in developing, commissioning, and sending their own members both locally and globally, often in partnership with other churches or agencies, and continuing to encourage, support, and advocate for them while making disciples cross-culturally.

Paul passed through the inland country and came to Ephesus...and he reasoned daily in the hall of Tyrannus. This continued for two years, so that all the residents of Asia heard the word of the Lord, both Jews and Greeks, Acts 19:1, 9-10

Ephesus was a crazy missions hub. Yes, Paul lectured there five hours a day for two years, but as John Calvin commented, "Luke does not mean that the people who lived in Asia came there to hear Paul, but that the effect of his preaching spread."[1] However, the wonder of this gospel movement really isn't measured by an entire region hearing the gospel. Instead, "it was during this time that the seven churches named in Revelation 2-3, as well as many others, came into being."[2] And these great churches became outposts for the gospel: "Once Paul had established churches he also drew them into his missionary strategy by using them as bases for the extension of the gospel into the surrounding neighborhoods and the world."[3] God did a vast work through the great sending church at Ephesus.

But according to Jesus, only forty years later, the same church was nothing.

But this I have against you, that you have abandoned the love you had at first. Remember therefore from where you have fallen; repent, and do the works you did at first. If not, I will come to you and remove your lampstand from its place, unless you repent, Revelation 2:4-5

Is it too harsh to say that Ephesus had become nothing? Not if we remember Paul's love chapter: "if I have not love, I am nothing" (1 Corinthians 13:2). Ouch. So what can we learn? Surely Ephesus' story serves as an example to us. How is a church to send and keep sending, to stay vibrantly active in the mission of God? Answering that involves a much bigger issue. C. S. Lewis has famously spoken to it:

Our Lord finds our desires not too strong, but too weak. We are half-hearted creatures, fooling about with drink and sex and ambition when infinite joy is offered us, like an ignorant child who wants to go on making mud pies in a slum because he cannot imagine what is meant by the offer of a holiday at the sea. We are far too easily pleased.[4]

Woe to our churches if missions itself becomes the object of our affection! Hear John Piper's first line in *Let the Nations Be Glad*: "Mission is not the ultimate goal of the church. Worship is."[5] The first step—and only hope—of being about sending is being about God. The Ephesians' work for missions grew mechanical because their love for God grew cold. "A truly Christian love," writes Jonathan Edwards, "is a humble broken-hearted joy, and leaves the Christian more poor in spirit, and more like a little child, and more disposed to a universal lowliness of behaviour."[6] It's this kind of love for God that can make our obedience bloody (John 14:15). Yet our task-driven culture and self-righteous nature leads us instead to love our bloody obedience.

Yes, the mark of a church is not its seating capacity but its sending capacity. Yet the measure of a church begins not with its sending as much as its worship. "At its heart, worship is rooted in love," the love of a great God that makes possible the love *for* a great God.[7] In an old sermon titled, "A Pastor's Role in World Missions," John Piper said poignantly,

Unless we take our starting point from the sovereign majesty of God and his ultimate allegiance to his own glory above all else, our missionary theology and strategy and motivation will become man-centered and will in the end degenerate into a powerless sentimentality...the most important thing pastors can do to arouse and sustain a passion for world evangelization is week in and week out to help their people see the crags and peaks and icy cliffs and snowcapped heights of God's majestic character.[8]

In this way pastors of sending churches help their people abide in Christ. Week after week they rehearse that we are indeed unworthy and inadequate for accomplishing God's grand mission.[9] And they aren't afraid to bring to mind that this mission and its glories didn't originate with us.[10] Yet as they bring the gospel home again and again, pastors deadbolt their churches' love and confidence in the God who has chosen them to bear much fruit, proving them to be his disciples (John 15:8).

What's a great first step? The original sending church at Antioch recommends "worshiping the Lord and fasting" (Acts 13:2). For a modern rendition I'll give the parting word to Pat Hood, a pastor who saw his church move from the sidelines to the playing field ("missions-minded to missional"[11]) through a Spirit-led church-wide call to fasting and prayer:

Since this awakening, [we] have been doing things we have never done before, all over the world... Everything started when we paused to seek the heart of God through prayer and fasting. It was then that he helped us to be something different so we could do something different for his glory.[12]

[1] John Calvin, *Acts* (Wheaton, IL: Crossway, 1995), 322.

[2] R. Kent Hughes, *Acts: The Church Afire* (Wheaton, IL: Crossway, 1996), 255.

[3] James Montgomery Boice, *Acts: An Expositional Commentary* (Grand Rapids, MI: Baker, 2006), 320; adapted from Roger S. Greenway.

[4] C. S. Lewis, *The Weight of Glory* (New York, NY: HarperCollins, 2001), 26.

[5] John Piper, *Let the Nations Be Glad: The Supremacy of God in Missions* (Grand Rapids, Baker Academic, 2010), 17.

[6] Jonathan Edwards, *A Treatise on Religious Affections* (Grand Rapids, MI: Baker, 1982).

[7] Mike Cosper, *Rhythms of Grace: How the Church's Worship Tells the Story of the Gospel* (Wheaton, IL: Crossway, 2013), 26.

[8] John Piper. (31 October 1984). *A Pastor's Role in World Missions*. Retrieved from http://www.desiringgod.org/conference-messages/a-pastors-role-in-world-missions.

[9] Greg Gilbert, *What is the Gospel?* (Wheaton, IL: Crossway, 2010), 119.

[10] Ross Hastings, *Missional God, Missional Church: Hope for Re-Evangelizing the West* (Downers Grove, IL: IVP Academic, 2012), 129.

[11] Ed Stetzer, *Planting Missional Churches: Planting a Church That's Biblically Sound ad Reaching People in Culture* (Nashville, TN: B&H Academic, 2006), 19.

[12] Pat Hood, *The Sending Church: The Church Must Leave the Building* (Nashville, TN: B&H Books, 2013), 117-118.

prayerful

A Sending Church is a local community of Christ-followers who have made a covenant together to be **prayerful**, deliberate, and proactive in developing, commissioning, and sending their own members both locally and globally, often in partnership with other churches or agencies, and continuing to encourage, support, and advocate for them while making disciples cross-culturally.

While at a secret meeting with house church leaders in an intensely persecuted region of China, missiologist Nik Ripken was asked a peculiar question: "Are the believers [in other countries] persecuted like we are?" Ripken answered yes, describing the kind of persecution taking place in two Middle Eastern countries. The group became eerily silent. Early the next morning Ripken was jarred awake to shouts and screams. It wasn't secret police, but the Chinese Christians praying in anguish for their Middle Eastern brothers and sisters. Ripken comments, "In that instant, I could see why the number of Chinese believers had gone from a few hundred thousand to perhaps hundreds of millions!"[1]

Prayer is the church's fuel for mission. E.M. Bounds said that without prayer "the church is lifeless and powerless."[2] Yet it's not a stretch to say that when she does pray, the earth shakes—just look at the examples strewn throughout the book of Acts! The first church devoted themselves to prayer, which was followed by awe upon everyone, many wonders and signs, having all things in common, and the daily addition of new believers (2:42-47). Later, in response to persecution, the church prayed together for boldness, which led to a mini earthquake, the filling of the Holy Spirit, and continued daring witness (4:23-31). The leaders of the church at Antioch fasted and prayed together, and the Holy Spirit told them to send out Barnabas and Saul, sparking a massive gospel movement (13:1-3). As Donald Whitney puts it, "united prayer is always linked with the effectiveness of the gospel and the church."[3]

Sending churches recognize that the neighborhoods and the nations are theirs for the asking.[4] This is because the neighborhoods and nations belong to the one who has all authority in heaven and on earth (Matthew 28:18), who rules over them with a rod of iron (Psalm 2:9), and who is obliged to share the throne with his own people (2 Timothy 2:12). Prayer is "a wartime walkie-talkie for the mission of the church".[5] As the church battles on the front lines against the powers of darkness and unbelief, she is maneuvered, provisioned, and made victorious by God through prayer.

Thankfully, Jesus knows well our busy ambitions, and he is fit to remind us constantly of our need. He remarks in Luke 10:2 that the "harvest is plentiful, but the laborers are few." There, seventy-two eager young disciples are lining up like a fifth grade 100-yard dash, ready to impress the Messiah with their skills. Yet notice that Jesus' first command isn't go. Instead he says *pray*—"Pray earnestly to the Lord of the harvest to send out laborers into his harvest." The implication wasn't that praying was more pious than going, but that they needed Jesus every step of the way. He would later warn them, "When you have done all that you were commanded, say, 'We are unworthy servants; we have only done what was our duty,'" (17:10). The call to be prayerful is not an obligation to rote activity as though we're spinning Buddhist prayer wheels, but a call to know Christ. Said Dallas Willard, "An obsession merely with doing what God commands may be the very thing that rules out being the kind of person that he calls us to be."[6]

When viewed in light of who God is, the command to pray becomes both a powerful weapon and a warm invitation. In a sending church it is every person's entry point into the mission. The old adage is true, every Christian can change the world through prayer. But what an individualistic perspective! Medal of Honor recipients may turn battles, but armies win wars. The unified prayer of a church is a force few of us have ever witnessed outside the Scriptures. The church will rally to causes, campaigns, and cantatas, but just try to get everyone together to pray for an hour. Insert cricket sounds.

Mission leaders, especially pastors, can lead the way in shaping a culture of prayerfulness. D.A. Carson notes that Charles Spurgeon surprisingly was willing to share his pulpit, but not his "pastoral prayer," which was intended to "not only intercede with God but also instruct and edify and encourage the saints."[7] Here the church will learn how to cry out for the neighborhoods and the nations rather than simply asking God to 'bless the missionaries'.[8]

But prayer is not merely the entry point of missions in a sending church. It's the foundation for every element of sending. What will be the church's strategy? Who will lead in its formation? How will the church develop missionaries? Where will missionaries be sent? Who will the church partner with? What will ongoing support look like? Looks like we've got a lot to be praying about.

---

[1] Nik Ripken and Gregg Lewis, *The Insanity of God: A True Story of Faith Resurrected* (Nashville, TN: B&H Books, 2013), 243-244.
[2] E. M. Bounds, *The Complete Works of E. M. Bounds on Prayer* (Grand Rapids, MI: Baker, 1990), 75.
[3] Donald S. Whitney, *Spiritual Disciplines Within the Church: Participating Fully in the Body of Christ* (Chicago, IL: Moody, 1996), 167.
[4] Jason Mandryk, *Operation World: The Definitive Prayer Guide to Every Nation* (Downers Grove, IL: IVP Books, 2010), xxii.
[5] John Piper, *Let the Nations Be Glad: The Supremacy of God in Missions* (Grand Rapids, Baker Academic, 2010), 45.
[6] Dallas Willard, *Hearing God: Developing a Conversational Relationship with God* (Downers Grove, IL: IVP Books, 1999) 12.
[7] D. A. Carson, *A Call to Spiritual Reformation: Priorities from Paul and His Prayers* (Grand Rapids, MI: Baker Academic, 1992).
[8] Mike Barnett, ed., *Discovering the Mission of God: Best Missional Practices for the 21st Century* (Downers Grove, IL: IVP Academic, 2012), 372.

deliberate

> A Sending Church is a local community of Christ-followers who have made a covenant together to be prayerful, **deliberate**, and proactive in developing, commissioning, and sending their own members both locally and globally, often in partnership with other churches or agencies, and continuing to encourage, support, and advocate for them while making disciples cross-culturally.

They drew a line in the sand. That's the pivotal moment in the nonfiction account (and 2013 film) titled *Lone Survivor* by Marcus Luttrell, the last living member of Seal Team 10. This brutal story follows Operation Redwing into the mountains of Afghanistan where four Navy SEALS were tasked with killing al Qaeda leader, Ahmad Shah. Plans went awry when the team encountered goat herders and were forced to kill them or let them go—exposing their position to an army of al Qaeda assassins. The team's leader made the hard, right call and within moments of the herders' release all hell broke loose. Luttrell captures the theme of the moment this way: "We train for war and fight to win. I stand ready to bring the full spectrum of combat power to bear in order to achieve my mission".[1] The call had been made. The rest is history.

There comes a time when every church must draw a line in the sand. *Are we going to be on mission or* let someone else do it for us? This is the inconvenient fork in the road. John Stott wrote, "We must be global Christians with a global vision because our God is a global God...His authority and presence leaves no choice."[2] This implication is that a "church that does not center itself on obedience to our Lord's Great Commission is a church in significant sin."[3] The days of Christendom are over, so the mere presence of churches is not enough to attract people to the gospel.[4] "Christian presence in itself does not exhaust the biblical concept of being sent...Christ was more than mere presence."[5] His life on mission, which now fills every church that belongs to him, finishes off our hesitancy Mortal Combat-style.[6] He has made a way for his church to be deliberate in sending.

One of the places this is most beautifully pictured is the momentous shift midway into Luke's Gospel: "When the days drew near for him to be taken up, he set his face to go to Jerusalem" (9:51). Philip Graham Ryken unpacks what exactly this meant:

What Jesus suffered was not some unfortunate accident, but the direct result of his deliberate obedience to his divine calling as Savior of the world...When Jesus set his face toward Jerusalem, therefore, he was looking ahead to the cross and to the crown that he would gain by dying for sinners. Once he fixed his gaze in that direction, he would never look back. Nothing would deter him or distract him from doing what he was called to do, *the work that was his everlasting destiny and that he desired to do for our salvation.[7]*

Jesus paid the price for our feet-dragging. It is the authority of the resurrected Christ in the Person of the Spirit that empowers the church to draw a line in the sand. Because Jesus set his face toward Jerusalem, our faces may be set toward Jerusalem, Judea, Samaria, and the ends of the earth. They must be.

What does it look like to be deliberate? Pastor David Horner has a boatload to say about that in his book, *When Missions Shapes the Mission: You and Your Church Can Reach the World*. After remarking that 88% of churches (Southern Baptist) never themselves raise up and send a missionary, he points the finger back on himself, noting that the greatest hurdle is "pastors—uninspired, uninvolved, uninformed". He doesn't say this to condemn pastors who are already drained to the dregs shepherding their homes and churches while seeking to also engage their neighborhood, but to remind them of their privilege in being lead repent-ers. The pastor's heart will always be reflected in his congregation, for better or worse.[8]

This does not mean, however, that the entire burden weighs solely on the pastor. It would be funny to watch two head coaches go at it one on one, but it's a team game.[9] Pastor Tim Keller spends a big chunk of *Center Church* emphasizing that missional church isn't possible without missional community. The church "trains and encourages its people to be in mission," then equips them "both for evangelistic witness and for public life and vocation."[10] But this process doesn't offer a next-day delivery option. Rather, the church as a bride must be honored, affirmed, wooed, and waited upon to give herself to Christ and own his mission for her.[11]

The kind of missional imagination it takes to lead the church deliberately *cannot* come from the pastor alone.[12] Surveying over one hundred churches for best missions practices, Horner gives the number one slot to "assigning clear leadership responsibility for missions (someone devoted to that effort)."[13] Thabiti Anyabwile adds that every church should ask, "Does the staffing pattern in my church reflect an emphasis on the Great Commission (missions) or an emphasis on local programming (maintenance)?"[14] How is your church going to develop, commission, send, partner, encourage, support, and advocate? What person(s), whether staff or volunteer, will develop the battle plan?

It's the pivotal moment.

¹ Marcus Luttrell and Patrick Robinson, *Lone Survivor: The Eyewitness Account of Operation Redwing and the Lost Heroes of SEAL Team 10* (New York, NY: Back Bay Books, 2007).

² John Stott, *Basic Christianity* (Grand Rapids, MI: Eerdmans, 2012).

³ Thabiti Anyabwile. (18 March 2014). *Being a Missions-Centered Local Church: Lessons from Johnson Ferry Baptist Church.* Retrieved from http://www.thegospelcoalition.org/blogs/thabitianyabwile/2014/03/18/being-a-missions-centered-local-church-lessons-from-johnson-ferry-baptist-church/.

⁴ Tim Chester and Steve Timmis, *Everyday Church: Gospel Communities on Mission* (Wheaton, IL: Crossway, 2012), 13-35.

⁵ George W. Peters, *A Biblical Theology of Missions* (Chicago, IL: Moody, 1984), 212.

⁶ YouTube. (14 February 2007). *Mortal Kombat 1 Fatalities.* Retrieved from https://www.youtube.com/watch?v=BPylK_Vnbl4.

⁷ Philip Graham Ryken, *Luke* (Philipsburg, NJ: P&R Publishing, 2009), 497-498.

⁸ David Horner, *When Missions Shapes the Mission: You and Your Church Can Reach the World* (Nashville, TN: B&H Books, 2011), 21, 30.

⁹ Tony Moss. (18 March 2014). *Ranking the NCAA Tournament Coaches by Playing Career, 1-68.* Retrieved from http://www.cbssports.com/collegebasketball/eye-on-college-basketball/24490175/ranking-the-ncaa-tournament-coaches-by-playing-career-1-68.

¹⁰ Timothy Keller, *Center Church: Doing Balanced, Gospel-Centered Ministry in Your City* (Grand Rapids, MI: Zondervan, 2012), 19-21.

¹¹ George Miley, *Loving the Church, Blessing the Nations: Pursuing the Role of Local Churches in Global Mission* (Downers Grove, IL: IVP Books, 2005), 68.

¹² Alan Roxburgh and Fred Romanuk, *The Missional Leader: Equipping Your Church to Reach a Changing World* (Indianapolis, IN: Jossey-Bass, 2006), 146.

¹³ Horner, *When Missions Shapes the Mission,* 140.

¹⁴ Anyabwile, *Being a Missions-Centered Local Church.*

proactive

A Sending Church is a local community of Christ-
followers who have made a covenant together to be
prayerful, deliberate, and **proactive** in developing,
commissioning, and sending their own members
both locally and globally, often in partnership with
other churches or agencies, and continuing to
encourage, support, and advocate for them while
making disciples cross-culturally.

A pastor of over thirty-five years sat down with a group of eager seminary students. Expecting to glean finely aged insight about how to make it in the big leagues, each young man closed out Twitter long enough to take a note or two. The pastor began, "A woman tripped over a cord in our church and sued us for damages. Even though we have a video showing that she didn't even fall down, she won $30,000. You want to be in ministry? Better learn to protect yourself." And back to Twitter they went.

Though the pastor touched on a real dynamic of ministry in today's world, his pressing concern didn't quite capture God's life-giving intention for his people. Is the church meant merely to be on the defensive? Does she just hole up in the fort and react to enemy advances? Is her commission championed by waiting to give half-cocked answers when questions arise? Drawing a line in the sand and being all in when it comes to sending still may leave the church ultimately shortsighted. If it is to be a sending church, it will have to be proactive. By definition that means it will "control situations by making things happen".[1]

Easy, bossy pants, isn't that God's job?

Precisely. The church can be proactive because God is proactive. Passages like Matthew 24:14 among others (Genesis 3:15, Isaiah 49:6, John 6:37-39, Romans 8:29, Ephesians 1:4-5, Revelation 7:9) show just how ahead of the game God is: "And this gospel of the kingdom will be proclaimed throughout the whole world as a testimony to all nations, then the end will come." The thrill of mission is not that it might succeed, but that it will succeed. Kevin DeYoung says this is (surprisingly) our great motivator for sending.[2] Daniel Akin and Bruce Riley Ashford add,

God himself defines, organizes, empowers, and ultimately accomplishes Christian mission. Based upon this truth and the confidence it engenders, we seek to...proclaim and embody the gospel, making it readily accessible to every tribe, tongue, people, and nation...Our task is daunting...however, [it] is matched and exceeded by the magnitude of our biblical convictions...that God has promised and will secure the final triumph of his gospel, even to the ends of the earth.[3]

It's a good thing the church is offered such confidence because no task is more endemic to the church—nor more difficult—than relating the gospel to human cultures.[4] Acts 17:26-27 reveals that God has shaped the seemingly meaningless details of every culture so that people "should seek God, and perhaps feel their way toward him and find him." This means that there are inherit aspects of every culture that the church can use to relate the gospel in ways people can understand. "The Spirit is already at work ahead of the church!"[5] Like the Army Corps of Engineers, the Spirit builds these bridges for us to march across and take the offensive. But if the church has the upper hand and the outcome is sure, why is it that, as William Carey questioned in his own day, "multitudes sit at their ease, and give themselves no concern about the far greater part of their fellow-sinners, who to this day are lost in ignorance and idolatry"?[6]

Part of the answer is that our world is crazy complex. Globalization. Populization. Pluralization. Migration. Pornification. It's downright mayhem. Why not leave it to the professionals? Because,

it is incumbent upon every Christian and every church to be aware of the issues, opportunities, challenges, and obstacles that we face in the eventual accomplishment of the Great Commission. If we are going to obediently and meaningfully impact the world around us with the gospel that has been entrusted to us, then we must be cognizant of what God is sovereignly doing around the world and how God is graciously calling us to join with Him in the work.[7]

Sending churches continually wrestle to avoid misreading Scripture and the world through Western eyes.[8] Pick up any book on current global missions issues and you'll quickly see the urgent theme that churches "can remain relevant only to the extent that they read, listen, and interact with believers from around the world."[9] What does it mean for the church that the "center of gravity in the Christian world has shifted inexorably southward to Africa, Asia, and Latin America"?[10] Churches that stay on top of things already realize they must "no longer be the leaders, the initiators, the norm setters, [but instead] the helpers, the assistants, and the facilitators."[11]

It's always risky to predict the future, but two things are sure: God will complete his mission and he'll do it through his people.[12] His proactive people, that is.

[1] Merriam-Webster Dictionary. (2014). *Proactive*. Retrieved from http://www.merriam-webster.com/dictionary/proactive.

[2] Kevin DeYoung. (2013). *Five Surprising Motivations for Missions*. Retrieved from http://crosscon.com/media/2014/01/five-surprising-motivations-for-mission-session-iii/.

[3] Bruce Riley Ashford, Ed., *Theology and Practice of Mission: God, the Church, and the Nations* (Nashville, TN: B&H Academic, 2011), 333; see Ashford and Daniel Akin's chapter, "A Challenge for Our Churches".

[4] Paul G. Hiebert, *Anthropological Insights for Missionaries* (Grand Rapids, MI: Baker Academic, 1986), 29.

[5] Ross Hastings, *Missional God, Missional Church: Hope for Re-Evangelizing the West* (Downers Grove, IL: IVP Academic, 2012), 304-305.

[6] William Carey, *An Enquiry into the Obligations of Christians, to Use Means for the Conversion of the Heathens* (Leicester: Anne Ireland, 1792), 7-8.

[7] J. D. Payne, *Pressure Points: Twelve Global Issues Shaping the Face of the Church* (Nashville, TN: Thomas Nelson, 2013), xii; see Platt's foreword.

[8] E. Randolph Richards and Brandon J. O'Brien, *Misreading Scripture with Western Eyes: Removing Cultural Blindness to Better Understand the Bible* (Downers Grove: IL, IVP Books, 2012).

[9] Michael Pocock, Gailyn van Rheenen, and Douglas McConnell, *The Changing Face of Missions: Engaging Contemporary Issues and Trends* (Grand Rapids, MI: Baker Academic, 2005), 14.

[10] Philip Jenkins, *The Next Christendom: The Coming of Global Christianity* (Oxford: Oxford Press, 2002), 1-3.

[11] Paul Borthwick, *Western Christians in Global Mission: What's the Role of the North American Church?* (Downers Grove: IVP Books, 2012), 87; quote is taken from Andrew Walls.

[12] A. Scott Moreau, *Contextualization in World Missions: Mapping and Assessing Evangelical Models* (Grand Rapids, MI: Kregel Publications, 2012), 315.

in developing

A Sending Church is a local community of Christ-followers who have made a covenant together to be prayerful, deliberate, and proactive **in developing**, commissioning, and sending their own members both locally and globally, often in partnership with other churches or agencies, and continuing to encourage, support, and advocate for them while making disciples cross-culturally.

Developing missionaries is a beast. That's why we're going to try taming it in three phases: identification, assessment, development.

Identification

Over twenty years ago I joined the Royal Ambassadors (RA's), a missions discipleship program for boys in grades 1-6. It was great. We camped and played basketball and made boxcars. I loved it so much that my leaders called me "the general" because I made it through all the workbooks and earned every possible badge you could imagine. But as great a church boy scout as I was, I never sensed any grand missionary call. I don't remember learning much about God's mission, in fact. Nor a lot about the gospel.

Is this the best churches have to offer when it comes to developing missionaries?

Thankfully, the general still ended up with a sense of mission, not through a program, but via the age-old missionary factory: the transforming power of the gospel, the compelling call of the word and Spirit, and the deal-sealing affirmation of the body of Christ. Programs, agencies, conferences, books, and websites are great contributors to the development of missionaries, but none should hold a candle to "the household of God, which is the church of the living God, a pillar and buttress of the truth" (1 Timothy 3:15)—a quote which comes at the end of Paul's description of key identifiers in young potential leaders.

And that's really where development begins: identification. Identification at its core means recognizing that "God calls every Christian to live with a missionary heart."[1] With this perspective suddenly every boy in RA's really is a potential future missionary, not depending on his surrender to a missionary call, but rather his surrender to the call of Christ. For Jesus never says, 'Come!' without saying 'Go!' That alone should have massive implications for how the sending church rolls. Preaching, teaching, and strategy should reflect the weight and wonder of every believer's commission to their home, neighborhood, classroom, and cubicle.

When full grown, identification also means the recognition of those with the apostolic capacity for being sent out to start new works, often internationally. George Miley addresses this element of identification in a helpful spirit:

Think for a moment how much initiating energy is still needed to fill the earth "with the knowledge of the glory of the Lord as the waters cover the sea" (Hab. 2:14). We need to initiate among the nations, within our own countries, cities, neighborhoods, and churches. Let's anticipate that there are far more of these called-and-gifted-by-God leaders than we might initially imagine.[2]

God is faithfully supplying himself with laborers to bring in his harvest. But what in the world do these potential missionaries look like? Before we kid ourselves by trying to answer that in a chapter, we first need the church to feel its responsibility in *figuring it out* together. No matter how many books you pick up on the topic, the bottom line is that it's often hard to discern. And hard decisions are best kept in the family, among those who know each other best. Mission agencies have in some ways professionalized identification and brought great insight to the table, but the spiritual authority to make such decisions has always rested with the church.

The biblical model also showcases a theme of identifying new leaders. Bruce Carlton highlights

Barnabas and Paul as prime examples of patrolling for potential: Barnabas' affirmation of newly-converted Paul (Acts 9:19-30), Paul's identification of young Timothy (Acts 16:1-3), and both Barnabas and Paul's raising up of elders in every church (Acts 14:23), just to name a few.[3] Greater still, however, is the very example of our Lord, who "went out on a mountain to pray, and all night continued in prayer to God" before identifying the twelve apostles in whom he would invest his life (Luke 6:12-13). If identification of leaders was that important and that challenging for the Son of God, what about us whose busied attempts at international missionary identification is sometimes little more than scanning for church members with Chacos[4] and Nalgenes[5]?!

The culture of a sending church creates a two-way street of identification. As church leaders proactively equip an entire body of missionaries, they are also on the lookout for the international goers; as church members deliberately grow in their identity as missionaries, they bring their desire for new works beyond the church's context to their leaders. The key here is not process but relationship, life on life investment, which helps avoid separating "the mission of the church from the missionaries of the church."[6]

Developing through identification means recognizing Christ in every believer. Whether RA or PhD, chances are there's a missionary or two just waiting to be developed.

Assessment

When Sheikh Mohammed bin Rashid Al Maktoum said that he wanted to put Dubai on the map with something really sensational, he wasn't joking. Only a few years later he baffled the world with a true modern marvel, the Burj Khalifa. To call it the world's tallest building is an understatement. The last time I flew out of Dubai, after more than a minute of ascent I was still looking up at the monstrous tower. Too bad Dubai bit off more than they could chew and ended up bailed out for $10 billion by their neighbor, Abu Dhabi, not to mention that for several months most offices and apartments in the Burj were left as empty as Dubai's pockets.[7] Ouch.

Such contemporary matters are ironically reminiscent of a pertinent old teaching. In Luke 14:28-30 Jesus said, "For which of you, desiring to build a tower, does not first sit down and count the cost, whether he has enough to complete it? Otherwise, when he has laid a foundation and is not able to finish, all who see it begin to mock him." We know, of course, this wasn't spoken to poke at an ambitious leader, but to relate in a way we could understand the necessity of counting the cost in being Jesus' disciples. The sending church seeks to fulfill the Great Commission not by making logo-centric converts, but *Logos*-centric disciples who observe everything Jesus commanded. It issues the gospel call to come along with the missionary call to go.

72

Or does it?

Western churches typically assess new believers by calling them to profess their faith before the church, where it *counts*. Conversely, many global churches expect them to profess it outside the church, where it *costs*. The Bible calls for both. And according to Jesus, that's where assessment begins. He continued after the tower analogy, "If salt has lost its taste...it is thrown away" (Luke 14:34-35). Sending churches unapologetically expect all legitimate believers to be commissioned heralds of their great salvation. Even before membership class or evangelism training.

Thus the church, says Neal Pirolo, is "the ideal testing ground for potential missionaries."[8] As the church locally equips the entire congregation with missionary identity and practice, the Holy Spirit will, just as he did in Acts 13 with Paul and Barnabas, begin to draw out some as cross-cultural missionaries to be sent out to start new works. Developing them starts with identification, then moves to assessment. Though the sending church encourages everyone in their call to mission, "church selectivity" is crucial when it comes to those wrestling with an apostolic desire to start something new across town or across cultures. This means following the biblical pattern of selectively and collectively confirming an individual's sense of call to be sent. Any church that outsources the assessment of their cross-cultural missionary candidates "indicates a lack of understanding of the central role of the local church in world missions." In other words,

The most that an individual can do is express his willingness. Others must determine his worthiness. The individual may be free to go, but only his church knows if he is really fitted to go.[9]

Veteran missionary Thomas Hale echoes that the often strong-willed missionary candidate cannot rightly call for independence, for "the sending church must share in this call; they have the duty to examine the call and modify it as necessary."[10] If this is a problem for the candidate then the assessment may have already proven its point, for "a high view of, and a deep loyalty to, the church of Jesus Christ" is an indispensable missionary trait.[11]

However, may the church act worthily of such holy submission! Plurality in assessment applies as much to the church as to the candidate. David Harley nails it in *Training for Cross-Cultural Mission*: "The final evaluation of a [candidate] should not be left to one person. If possible, it should be discussed by all… [they] will have a broader perspective on strengths and weaknesses and will produce a more balanced assessment."[12]

This includes partnership with the missions agency, who with its experience and expertise "ought to be the church's provision, instrument, and arm to efficiently expedite her task." After all, continues Peters, "the church and not the missions agency...is God's authority and creation for sending forth missionaries."[13]

What's it look like practically? One safe bet is to start with scriptural models of assessment, such as the qualifications for elders and deacons in 1 Timothy 3 and Titus 1.[14] Another helpful guide is to think in categorical terms, such as knowing, being, doing[15] or calling, character, chemistry[16] or character, competence, calling[17]. Vulnerability is key. Only when candidates get real about their strengths and weaknesses can true assessment happen. And robust assessment opens the door for great development.

Development

None of us are born studs. Just ask 77 year-old Art Sherman, the trainer of the 2014 Kentucky Derby's champion thoroughbred, California Chrome. He was tasked with training the horse whose $8,000 mother seemed such a waste that his owners called themselves DAP (Dumbass Partners). Who would've thought such a long shot would land them with the roses at the world's greatest horserace? One converted doubter said afterward, "You don't train a horse like that, a California-bred, and get lucky and win the Kentucky Derby."[18] Apparently Sherman, with 23 years of jockey experience himself, knew just what it would take.

Development.

The Bible doesn't hide the worst about us, that "together [we] have become worthless" (Romans 3:12). As ones "conceived in sin" (Psalm 51:5), we have no claim to good pedigree. We don't need a good trainer, we need a Savior who grew up in all the ways we were meant to, "yet did not sin" (Hebrews 4:15). The kind of development due us starts with quitting all our training regimens, and surrendering to the only one who can bring us to "mature manhood, the measure of the stature of the fullness of Christ" (Ephesians 4:13).

This gospel is the church's greatest tool in developing missionaries. Preach it and live it and watch minds blow. But if you want minds to *stay* blown over Christ, enough to make life-long multipliers of missionaries to every nook, neighbor, and nation, the training ground isn't just your pews. Really, it's homes. Authors like Timothy Paul Jones,[19] Randy Stinson,[20] and Brian Haynes[21] have been calling churches back to the biblical idea of encouraging families as the primary disciplers of their children:

The apostles echoed assumptions in their epistles that Spirit-inspired authors had already woven throughout the Old Testament. In synagogues and Christian communities alike, this was not an optional focus for particularly ambitious parents. Training children in the fear of God represented nonnegotiable responsibility...For too many years, churches and parents have encouraged paid professionals to take the primary role in the discipleship of children.[22]

We've spoken earlier of missions agencies taking a posture of support toward the church. Here, the church itself must take such a posture toward parents. That's what Paul is talking about in Ephesians 4:11-12: "And [God] gave the apostles, the prophets, the evangelists, the shepherds and teachers, to equip the saints for the work of ministry, for building up the body of Christ". "Churches cannot provide what families neglect," says pastor David Horner.[23] But also families cannot easily reclaim what churches usurp. Developing missionaries happens in the proper partnership of the church empowering the home.

Turning discipleship over to church 'professionals' is actually just reflective of "the professionalization of everyone". Sociologist Harold L. Wilensky made this observation and coined the phrase in the 60's, noting "that an increasing number of full-time occupations were seeking to become recognized as professions" which would be marked by "autonomous expertise".[24] In other words, every 'trade' from making duck calls to breakup coaching began developing their own professionals, training, and jargon. David Hesselgrave applies the same effects to Christian missions. The result: the professionalization of missionaries and agencies who are often attracted to the missionary "trade" in search of self- and career-fulfillment.[25]

Now, of course, missions as a career isn't all bad. But it may unknowingly be helping us settle for less. Which is better: the commissioning of a few professionals, or the unleashing of an army of everyday missionaries forged in the church and home?

Umm...yes.

Yes, the church equips every member to be a missionary. And yes, the church equips some to leave to start new works. And it's all a glorious wreck of development that takes the entire church. The Holy Spirit forms missionaries[26] through discipling parents, preaching/worshiping/praying pastors, loving counselors, sharpening teachers, questioning coaches, returning missionaries, encouraging/challenging small group members, serving administrators, imagining children, admonishing seniors, persevering sufferers, wondering new believers, and a host of other parts of the body of Christ. And like Paul's time in Arabia (Acts 9:30, 11:25), missionaries are refined most by growing in cultural intelligence and sharing the gospel where they are.[27] So pick up *Tradecraft* and start practicing together.[28] Connect with a sending church to see how they develop missionaries. Order *Transformissional Coaching* and take a few budding leaders under your wing.[29] Get a resource like

Skills, Knowledge, Character and dream up your church's development process.[30]

It's your church's time to go for the roses. Identify. Assess. Develop.

---

[1] M. David Sills, *The Missionary Call: Find Your Place in God's Plan for the World* (Chicago, IL: Moody Publishers, 2008), 55.
[2] George Miley, *Loving the Church, Blessing the Nations: Pursuing the Role of Local Churches in Global Mission* (Downers Grove, IL: IVP Books, 2005), 110.
[3] Mike Barnett, Ed., *Discovering the Mission of God: Best Missional Practices for the 21st Century* (Downers Grove, IL: IVP Academic, 2012), 504; see R. Bruce Carlton's chapter, "Multiplying Leaders on Mission with God".
[4] http://www.chacos.com
[5] http://www.nalgene.com
[6] Scott Thomas and Tom Wood, *Gospel Coach: Shepherding Leaders to Glorify God* (Grand Rapids, MI: Zondervan, 2012), 62.
[7] The Economist Online. (29 December 2010). *Debt Forgetfulness.* Retrieved from http://www.economist.com/node/17800215.
[8] Neal Pirolo, *Serving as Senders - Today* (San Diego, CA: Emmaus Road International, 2012), 56.
[9] Paul A. Beals, *A People for His Name: A Church-Based Missions Strategy* (Pasadena, CA: William Carey Library, 2013), 86-87; quote is taken from Michael Griffiths.
[10] Thomas Hale, *On Being a Missionary* (Pasadena, CA: William Carey Library, 2012), 19.
[11] George W. Peters, *A Biblical Theology of Missions* (Chicago, IL: Moody Publishers, 1984), 297.
[12] David Harley, *Preparing to Serve: Training for Cross-Cultural Mission* (Pasadena, CA: William Carey Library, 2012), 120.

[13] Peters, *A Biblical Theology of Missions*, 229.

[14] Sojourn International. (2010). *Self-Assessment*. Retrieved from http://international.sojournchurch.com/?page_id=4443.

[15] Ibid.

[16] Larry McCrary. *The Sending Process*. Retrieved from http://theupstreamcollective.org/media/Sending_Assessment.pdf.

[17] Brad House, *Community: Taking Your Small Group Off Life Support* (Wheaton, IL: Crossway, 2011).

[18] Jennie Rees. (5 May 2014). *Kentucky Derby: California Chrome Shines Bright*. Retrieved from http://www.courier-journal.com/story/sports/horses/triple/derby/2014/05/03/kentucky-derby/8659903/.

[19] Timothy Paul Jones, *Family Ministry Field Guide: How Your Church Can Equip Parents to Make Disciples* (Indianapolis, IN: Wesleyan Publishing House, 2011).

[20] Randy Stinson and Timothy Paul Jones, Ed., *Trained in the Fear of God: Family Ministry in Theological, Historical, and Practical Perspective* (Grand Rapids, MI: Kregel Academic, 2011).

[21] Brian Haynes, *Shift: What it Takes to Finally Reach Families Today* (Loveland, CO: Group Publishing, 2009).

[22] Stinson and Jones, *Trained in the Fear of God*, 16-17.

[23] David Horner, *Firmly Rooted, Faithfully Growing: Principle-Based Ministry in the Church* (Raleigh, NC: Providence Communications, 2003).

[24] Harold L. Wilensky, "The Professionalization of Everyone?" American Journal of Sociology. Issue 70 (1964): 137-158. Print.

[25] David J. Hesselgrave, *Paradigms in Conflict: 10 Key Questions in Christian Missions Today* (Grand Rapids, MI: Kregel Academic, 2005), 224.

[26] Roland Allen, *Missionary Principles—and Practice* (Cambridge, UK: Lutterworth Press, 2006), 30.

[27] Eckhard J. Schnabel, *Paul the Missionary: Relaties, Strategies, and Methods* (Downers Grove, IL: IVP Academic, 2008), 60-63.

[28] Larry E. McCrary, Caleb Crider, Wade Stephens, and Rodney Calfee, *Tradecraft: For the Church on Mission* (Portland, OR: Urban Loft Publishers, 2013).

[29] Steve Ogne and Tim Roehl, *Transformissional Coaching: Empowering Leaders in a Changing Ministry World* (Nashville, TN: B&H Books, 2008).

[30] Greg Carter, *Skills, Knowledge, Character: A Church-Based Approach to Missionary Candidate Preparation* (Valparaiso, IN: Turtle River Press, 2010).

commissioning

> A Sending Church is a local community of Christ-followers who have made a covenant together to be prayerful, deliberate, and proactive in developing, **commissioning**, and sending their own members both locally and globally, often in partnership with other churches or agencies, and continuing to encourage, support, and advocate for them while making disciples cross-culturally.

I was wide-eyed when my friend nudged me and said, "He's from The People's Church in Toronto, one of the greatest missions churches in North America." Sitting across from us was Verdell Goulding, The People's global outreach director. He began sharing the story of his church and their missions-hearted founding pastor, Oswald J. Smith, which is recounted in the January 2014 issue of *Evangelical Missions Quarterly*.[1] To our surprise, however, the church with a $2 million missions budget supporting 379 global missionaries was in the midst of major realignment. For years they had commissioned just about anyone who wanted to do just about anything in just about any place, often with little connection to the church. They had shotgun-blasted themselves into being a *supporting* church, and are now on the hard road back to being a *sending* church. But what's the difference?

Much of it depends on commissioning. Does the church commission everyone or only some? When we speak of commissioning most of us think immediately of Matthew 28:18-20, the Great Commission. Ross Hastings, author of *Missional God, Missional Church*, points instead to the unique and equally rich version of Jesus' commission in John 20:19-23. There, the disciples were hopeless and desperate after Jesus' brutal death. Yet even more suddenly he appears in their midst with a word of peace, a commission, and a promise of the power to back it up. Hastings says that the church throughout the ages has been no different. Apart from Christ it will always be bankrupt and frazzled at the vast mission before it, but with him it becomes an unstoppable force:

the church in union with the risen Christ by the Spirit's inbreathing [is] the missionary of God... [John] describes the breath of the last Adam, being breathed into the last Adam's race, the new humanity in Christ, the church, and anticipates all those who would be brought into its communion by means of its missional nature and action: "as the Father has sent me, I am sending you." John's is a commission with cosmic consequences[2]

A commission of cosmic consequences has to make for the sent-ness of every believer. This evidently played out in the life of the early church. Though the drama of Acts centers on apostolic missionary activity, we know historically that the wider church body tended to centralize in Jerusalem—that is, until they were forcefully dispersed. Mark Noll names the fall of Jerusalem as the first decisive moment in the history of Christianity.

The great turning point represented by the destruction of Jerusalem was to move Christianity outward, to transform it from a religion shaped in nearly every particular by its early Jewish environment into a religion advancing toward universal significance[3]

The spread of the gospel makes it undeniable that early believers understood and owned their sense of commission as "elect exiles" to "proclaim the excellencies of him who called [them] out of darkness into his marvelous light" (1 Peter 1:1, 2:9). The sending church of today will do well to help every member understand and own their commission. As I heard one inner city pastor recently remark, "We've got to stop looking at people as our projects and start seeing them as our missionaries."

Practically, commissioning begins with a commissioning of parents to disciple their own children. The famous missionary, John G. Paton, wrote of his parents as those who were the most used of God in shaping his understanding of Christ and his commission. His parents would later write to him that they had "laid [him] upon the altar, their first-born, to be consecrated, if God saw fit, as a Missionary of the Cross, and it has been their

83

constant prayer that [he] might be prepared, qualified, and led to this very decision".[4] Churches empower parents to make missionaries.

Yet commissioning also stretches as far as the public celebration and commitment of those called to be sent out in starting new cross-cultural works. This is presented most clearly in Barnabas and Saul's commissioning from the church at Antioch in Acts 13:1-4. As the church leaders were praying and fasting together, the Holy Spirit commanded them, "Set apart for me Barnabas and Saul for the work to which I have called them" (v. 2). It's important to note in verse 3 that *the church* "sent them off," while in verse 4 they were "sent out by the Holy Spirit". So which was it? Many would only be comfortable with saying both if it was clearly articulated that the Holy Spirit primarily sent them while the church secondarily sent, or merely affirmed the Spirit's sending. That would make sense—but that would miss the mark. It would fail to acknowledge the depth of just how much the church embodies the Holy Spirit: "In [Christ] you also are being built together into a dwelling place for God by the Spirit" (Ephesians 2:22). The dual sending in Acts 13 is important, or it wouldn't be mentioned. If the Spirit sends while the church only affirms, then the precedent should continue that sees missionaries approaching the church with an individualistic sense of calling and the church simply offering an obligatory head nod. However, if both the Spirit and the church sends, then commissioning begins with the church's submission to the Holy Spirit, not just the

84

individual's, and carries the weight of acting alongside him to commission. As we saw from The People's Church, however, this kind of commissioning is not for everyone. Only those who have been developed and affirmed by the church should be commissioned cross-culturally with the church's blessing and partnership.

Nearly "nothing is more exciting and energizing to the spiritual life of a local church than the sending out of its own sons and daughters into strategic roles fulfilling the Great Commission."[5]The act of commissioning itself should certainly involve tears and sadness, but also a feeling that *this is right.*[6] It involves the laying on of hands and prayer as exemplified in Acts 13:1-3, but isn't "a ceremonial requirement as much as an intimate pledge of support and partnership in mission."[7]

Sending churches are commissioning churches.

[1] Verdell Goulding. (2014). "Voices in the Local Church: A Passion for Souls: Our Continued Journey in Global Missions". *Evangelical Missions Quarterly,* vol. 50, no. 1.

[2] Ross Hastings, *Missional God, Missional Church: Hope for Re-Evangelizing the West* (Downers Grove, IL: IVP Academic, 2012), 23.

[3] Mark A. Noll, *Turning Points: Decisive Moments in the History of Christianity* (Grand Rapids, MI: Baker Academic, 2012), 27.

[4] John Gibson Paton, *The Story of John G. Paton Or Thirty Years Among South Sea Cannibals* (New York, NY: A.L. Burton Company, 1892), Kindle edition.

[5] Propempo International. (2013). *Get Over There! Get Your Church to Celebrate and Send You Out.* Retrieved from http://cross.propempo.com/8-get-over-there.html.

[6] George Miley, *Loving the Church, Blessing the Nations: Pursuing the Role of Local Churches in Global Mission* (Downers Grove, IL: IVP, 2005), 136.

[7] Craig Ott and Gene Wilson, *Global Church Planting: Biblical Principles and Best Practices for Multiplication* (Grand Rapids, MI: Baker Academic, 2011), 183.

sending their own members

A Sending Church is a local community of Christ-followers who have made a covenant together to be prayerful, deliberate, and proactive in developing, commissioning, and **sending their own members** both locally and globally, often in partnership with other churches or agencies, and continuing to encourage, support, and advocate for them while making disciples cross-culturally.

Let's take a moment to recap.

We kicked this whole thing off with our reasoning behind teasing out a word by word definition of the sending church, namely, that it's a biblical identity that deserves clarity. Rooted in the very nature of God, sent-ness applies to every believer. More than that, the *missio Dei* is channeled through God's grand missionary, the church. Any church, large or small, can be a sending church. But to embrace their God-given identity, they must take the lead in sending their people rather than outsourcing their God-given task. The church grows sent ones in the incubator of missional community, where they learn to follow Christ's mission daily, but also where they remain bound to one another through covenantal commitment. The gospel abounds as the church focuses on being God's sent ones rather than just busily doing his commands. The sending church is prayerful, intentional, and visionary as it leads its own into mission. Identifying, assessing, and developing, it recognizes and raises up a congregation of sent ones, which includes every believer, as well as those gifted to go cross-culturally. It keeps the mission before them, and publicly commissions those called to start new works cross-culturally.

Whew, aren't you glad for a *concise* definition?

The next phrase in the definition reads, "sending their own members". But isn't that what we've been talking about the entire way thus far? Yes—so do you see why there's such a need for clarification in the term "sending church"? Sending is so much more than a practice. In many ways it encapsulates what the church is all about—really, what God is all about.

During a recent visit to east Africa, my team and I met with a woman who had sent her children to an orphanage because she and her husband had contracted HIV. Her husband soon died and she gave up all hope of ever regaining her children. They were adopted by an Evangelical family from the US and eventually became believers themselves. The family gave us photos and letters to deliver to the birth mother during our trip. When we met the frail woman she wept as we told her that her children had not forgotten her. We also told her that she had made a great sacrifice in sending her children to the care of others, and that they had become a blessing to many people. In a similar way, we told her God had made a great sacrifice in sending his Son so that he would be a blessing to many people. As we continued telling the gospel story to the candid crowd of her relatives and neighbors, we sensed anew the weight and intimacy of sending away one of your own.

Paul twice uses the phrase, "we are members of one another" (Romans 12:5, Ephesians 4:25) to describe the church, the body of Christ. He wields it not only as commentary on the headship of Christ, but as motivation for building one another up through spiritual gifts and loving truthfulness. Clarified by church membership and missional community, being members of one another is actually just the natural result of believers brought into communion with the Triune God. All this to say, sending one of your own members in some ways should feel like sending one of your own body parts. Here lies a sweetness and an agony both of which point the church to longing for God in the new Jerusalem, where "he will dwell with them...and wipe away every tear from their eyes" (Revelation 21:3-4).

Being a sending church also involves tears that come from hard conversations and hard goodbyes. As church leaders develop where and how they will focus their limited resources for the sake of greater impact, strategic sending will mean saying no to many good things for the sake of saying yes to the best things. Who will be fully funded, partially funded, or not funded at all? What about those who simply aren't qualified to go cross-culturally? What do you do with those who don't share the church's vision, or only pretend to? How do you send members who take international job transfers? If the church is to lead out in sending, she'll unapologetically point her people in strategic directions. Seeking God's leadership in mission alongside the church is explicitly biblical (Acts 13:1-3), but sometimes people won't see it that way, and hard conversations may end in hard goodbyes.

But more often than not, when the church steps into her God-given role, the Holy Spirit unifies hearts and makes clear paths for her to send her own members.

both locally and globally

A Sending Church is a local community of Christ-followers who have made a covenant together to be prayerful, deliberate, and proactive in developing, commissioning, and sending their own members **both locally and globally**, often in partnership with other churches or agencies, and continuing to encourage, support, and advocate for them while making disciples cross-culturally.

A Holistic Mission

Think globally, act locally. Chances are, you've heard this trendy phrase lately. Chances also are, like me, you may not have realized that it's actually old school. According to *New Republic*, the formulaic jingle was whipped up in 1970 as a grassroots motivator for environmental action.[1] The implications were simple: care for your little piece of earth, and *viola!*—you've changed the world. Yet now there's a whole new twist on the mantra. In an age where Google and Facebook are looking into drones to provide internet access to the entire world, the local connection to the rest of the globe is growing at a maddening rate.[2] With a single click you can already act globally while sitting in your pajamas at home, which is reflected in Matt Perman's popular new book, *What's Best Next:*

I want to equip you to do good in radical, creative ways for the cause of missions, ending extreme poverty (it can be done!), and bringing justice to the oppressed. To do this you don't have to move to Africa but, because of technology, can be involved from right where you are.[3]

But here a question lingers. Where then does the church press in to mission? Does she think globally and act locally, focusing all resources on her context and hoping the butterfly effect touches the nations? Or does she think locally and act globally, channeling resources internationally and assuming her sheer presence is making a difference in the neighborhood? Certainly both local and global contexts are massive undertakings worthy of the church's best efforts. And certainly Jesus will understand if we choose one over the other, right?

Thankfully, the overwhelming challenges that churches face in sending their members both locally and globally are by divine design. Impossible tasks? Indeed! And ripe with a need for the only God who can achieve the impossible through his people—"to show that the surpassing power belongs to God and not to us" (2 Corinthians 4:7). The church is undoubtedly called to God's mission, and God's mission "leads us in triumphal procession, and through us spreads the fragrance of the knowledge of him *everywhere*"—locally and globally (2 Corinthians 2:14, emphasis mine).

From its inception my local church rehearsed the catchy refrain, "In the city, for the city".[4] It was a reminder of their desire to be deeply rooted in the heart of the city rather than planting a group of commuter Christians with little transformative presence. The founding group of twenty-something's were tired of "the Great Commission in reverse," and wondered what it would look like to be the church in their context.[5] In *They Like Jesus But Not the Church* author Dan Kimball emphasizes that for the sake of the often-misrepresented gospel, the church must see "itself as being missionaries, rather than having a missions department, and that we [must] see ourselves as missionaries right where we live."[6] The church must bloom where it's planted, so to speak. If the church isn't living out a sent identity in its immediate context, then global action is probably a cover-up for apathy.

Yet the balance can easily be misconstrued in the opposition direction:

A church can be missional and yet miss the breadth of the command of Christ to take the gospel to the nations. It can narrow its "mission" to local ministries, to its own congregational life, or various combinations of emphasis which may or may not include the threefold range of missions Jesus outlined in Acts 1:8—Jerusalem, Judea and Samaria, and the uttermost parts of the earth. Missions is not really biblical missions until it strategically and comprehensively embraces a plan to reach all those areas with the message of salvation through Jesus Christ.[7]

Sending starts in the neighborhoods and spills over to the nations. And this has always been reflected in God's intention for his people. One of "the most hotly debated" missiological issues of late has been the missionary nature of Israel.[8] Were they called by God to actively engage the nations around them, or to serve them by being holy and separate? To go or to *be*? Christopher Wright responds that from the call of Abraham in Genesis 12 "Israel came into existence as a people with a mission entrusted to them from God for the sake of...blessing the nations."[9] Whether or not they were supposed to go as centrifugal heralds of Yahweh, they had the huge responsibility of knowing God,[10] a knowledge that was rooted in Jerusalem, but intended to usher in a servant of such cosmic significance that it would be too narrow a task for him to only rescue Israel. Instead, he would be "a light for the nations, that salvation may reach to the end of the earth" (Isaiah 49:6). How much more, then, is his church called and equipped to participate in a seismic mission epicentered locally and tremoring globally!

A Unified Mission

So does that mean there two unique missions in different directions?

Mission, regardless of where it lands, flows from God and his church. Ed Stetzer comments that though the most impactful saints of history differed in their ideas and sometimes struggled with each other, all of them "had this in common: they advanced God's mission through Christ's church."[11] They simply followed Jesus as disciples do, and though he is rather mysterious in the specifics, he always leads his people into his fold and into his field. Paul showcases this truth in Ephesians 3, pointing out that the plan hidden for ages was that "through the church the manifold wisdom of God might now be made known," and it was "realized in Christ Jesus our Lord" (vv. 10-11). Why belabor the point? Because this is where local and global mission are entangled together, under one Lord, in one body. We'll constantly need this reminder, or we'll continually silo local mission and global mission as though they are distant relatives or dangerous rivals.

The fusion of local and global mission is a dream team in building up the body of Christ. Pastor Tim Keller comments in *Ministries of Mercy,*

The church is a living thing, and like all living things, its growth must be fully orbed, symmetrical. A child, for example, must grow in all parts of his body, in the head, the upper, and the lower body. If all the organs do not mature and grow, none of them can. In the same way, a local church must be growing in all aspects of its life.[12]

The "fully orbed" involvement of all church members in being true disciples who follow Christ into tough neighborhoods and hostile nations is a picture of Ephesians 4: "the whole body, joined and held together by every joint with which it is equipped, when each part is working properly, makes the body grow so that it builds itself up in love" (v. 16). As we learn from one another in our local and global efforts by joining together in our vision, strategy, and action, it's the entire church that benefits.

But this isn't for the church alone, as I was reminded this week by Josh Thomas and Nathan Ivey, pastors on the front lines of local missions engagement. They believe whole-heartedly that "the local church is God's vehicle for social change," and that we can set ourselves up for failure by trying solely to build up the church without reaching the city.[13] The synergy of local and global mission is meant to also benefit those around it, both near and far. "It's not 'In the city, for the city,'" said Thomas, "but 'In the city, with the city.' We've got to be more than advocates; we want to invite [the neighborhood] into the process." Sure, in the trenches the church will blossom. But shouldn't the trenches grow some flowers along the way too?

The one-two punch of local and global mission makes so much sense in building the church and blessing the world. So, as pastor Randy Pope asks, "why do we see ourselves in a defensive posture?"[14]

Maybe it's because we don't realize what we've got, just how much local and global mission inform and spur one another on. Consider these:

- It's hard to recognize that we have a unique culture of our own until we experience a foreign culture. Global mission "helps us step out of our own heads" and see spiritual realities locally (Thomas).

- Nothing can prepare global sent ones for the day-to-day grind like local mission. It's the classroom in which to mess up and seek forgiveness as well as experience setbacks and fall on God.[15]

- The nations are now all around us, so to be faithful locally will require global understanding and skills. Churches will have to "think and act like missionaries" in their own context.[16]

- The local church has the responsibility to test and approve before they appoint and send. Why would our churches want to send anyone globally who has not first proven themselves locally?[17]

- Today's global sent ones, whether church planters or executives or developers or students, will face a sea of complex problems.

How will they navigate them without having waded into local complexities beforehand?[18]

- Global mission in the West must rightly respond to no longer being the epicenter of Christianity. Sent ones will tend to lord over the global church unless they've already learned to serve and co-labor locally.[19]

- Local mission in the West is often driven by information rather than obedience, while global mission tends to forsake theological training for evangelistic fervor. They'll need each other to maintain a faithful balance.[20]

- The US now *receives* more missionaries than any country in the world. How will local mission leaders learn to welcome and partner with them without the experience and coaching of global mission leaders?[21]

---

[1] New Republic. (21 April 2014). *Earth Day: 'Think Globally, Act Locally' is Back*. Retrieved from http://www.newrepublic.com/article/117459/earth-day-2014-think-globally-act-locally-back.

[2] The Washington Post. (14 April 2014). *Google buys drone maker Titan Aerospace*. Retrieved from http://www.washingtonpost.com/blogs/the-switch/wp/2014/04/14/google-buys-drone-maker-titan-aerospace-2/.

[3] Matt Perman, *What's Best Next: How the Gospel Transforms the Way You Get Things Done* (Grand Rapids, MI: Zondervan, 2014), 20.

[4] Sojourn Community Church. *Our Story and Our Name*. Retrieved from http://sojournchurch.com/about-us/our-story-and-our-name/.

5 Darren Carlson. (27 June 2012). *Toward Better Short-Term Missions.* Retrieved from http://www.thegospelcoalition.org/article/toward-better-short-term-missions/.

6 Dan Kimball, *They Like Jesus But Not the Church: Insights from Emerging Generations* (Grand Rapids, MI: Zondervan, 2007).

7 David Horner, *When Missions Shapes the Mission: You and Your Church Can Reach the World* (Nashville, TN: B&H Books, 2011), 3.

8 Andreas J. Kostenberger and Peter T. O'Brien, *Salvation to the Ends of the Earth: A Biblical Theology of Mission* (Downers Grove, IL: IVP , 2001), 34.

9 Christopher J. H. Wright, *The Mission of God: Unlocking the Bible's Grand Narrative* (Downers Grove, IL: IVP Academic, 2006), 65.

10 Ibid., 66.

11 Mike Barnett, Ed., *Discovering the Mission of God: Best Missional Practices for the 21st Century* (Downers Grove, IL: IVP Academic, 2012, 598; see Ed Stetzer's chapter, "The Trouble with Our Jerusalems".

12 Timothy J. Keller, *Ministries of Mercy: The Call of the Jericho Road* (Philipsburg, NJ: P&R Publishing, 1997), 209.

13 SEED. (2013). *About.* Retrieved from http://seed.sojournchurch.com/about-us/.

14 Randy Pope, *The Intentional Church: Moving from Church Success to Community Transformation* (Chicago, IL: Moody Publishers, 2006), 25.

15 Harvie M. Conn and Manuel Ortiz, *Urban Ministry: The Kingdom, the City, and the People of God* (Downers Grove, IL: IVP Academic, 2010).

16 Larry E. McCrary, Caleb Crider, Wade Stephens, and Rodney Calfee, *Tradecraft: For the Church on Mission* (Portland, OR: Urban Loft Publishers, 2013).

17 Thomas Hale, *On Being a Missionary* (Pasadena, CA: William Carey Library, 2012).

18 Steve Corbett and Brian Fikkert, *When Helping Hurts: How to Alleviate Poverty Without Hurting the Poor...and Yourself* (Chicago, IL: Moody Publishers, 2014).

19 Paul Borthwick, *Western Christians in Global Mission: What's the Role of the North American Church?* (Downers Grove, IL: IVP Books, 2012).

20 M. David Sills, *Reaching and Teaching: A Call to Great Commission Obedience* (Chicago, IL: Moody Publishers, 2010).

21 Melissa Stephan. 25 July 2013). *The Surprising Countries Most Missionaries are Sent From and Go To.* Retrieved from http://www.christianitytoday.com/gleanings/2013/july/missionaries-countries-sent-received-csgc-gordon-conwell.html?paging=off.

often in partnership

A Sending Church is a local community of Christ-followers who have made a covenant together to be prayerful, deliberate, and proactive in developing, commissioning, and sending their own members both locally and globally, **often in partnership** with other churches or agencies, and continuing to encourage, support, and advocate for them while making disciples cross-culturally.

It was third grade field day. About 102 degrees. Stands packed. I stood with three of my best friends, ready to conquer the four-man relay. Three gold medals already hung around my neck from races earlier that day. Yeah, I was fast. And yeah, I ran with my medals on. Before taking my place as anchor, a horrifying reality set in—I was dependent on my team. They not only had to run fast, they had to keep from dropping the baton. "Whew," I said out loud. "Good thing *I'm* on this team."

Maybe this is why every time I think about teaming and partnership a relay race comes to mind. When we choose to partner, we choose to be dependent on one another. Partnership is a lovely idea, and like most components in the sending church definition, it's rooted in who God is. Indeed, he rules over the relay race of world history from start to finish—which only makes it that much more amazing that he allows us to carry *his* baton in *his* mission.

We see a couple dramatic instances of this in John's Gospel. The first, nestled in chapter 3, includes an often-overlooked story of John the Baptist. Deemed "the greatest man who had ever lived" by Jesus in Matthew 11:11, John's prominence in his day is hard for us to fully grasp. God was using him to single-handedly spark national revival as "all the country of Judea and Jerusalem were going out to him and were being baptized by him in the river Jordan, confessing their sins" (Mark 1:5). But when John's disciples pulled on his camel-hair pant leg and said, "look, Jesus is baptizing, and all are going to him" (John 3:26), the trending prophet faced a crisis: keep the baton or pass it on. Amazingly, by the Spirit who empowered him to be such a great man, John was overjoyed by Jesus' popularity and spoke the famous phrase, "He must increase, but I must decrease" (v. 30). He passed it on.

And there *was* One greater. A few chapters later Jesus was preparing his disciples for a truly mind-blowing pass of the baton. After announcing his certain exit from them, they were reeling with confusion. Then he explained why he was leaving, saying, "Truly, truly, I say to you, whoever believes in me will also do the works that I do; and greater works than these he will do, because I am going to the Father" (John 14:12). Jesus was passing the baton to his followers. They would be the anchor to finish off the race.

What's the point? God invites us to partner with him in his mission. Partnership is *his* principle. This is what Paul was getting at when he told the Corinthian church, "we are God's fellow workers" (1 Corinthians 3:9). Some of the believers had been giving credit for their church to Apollos, some to Peter, and some to Paul. Yet neither "he who plants nor he who waters is anything, but only God who gives the growth" (v. 7). We are partners with God and one another, a term applied insightfully by The Austin Stone Community Church:

Partners are the saints of God who do the work of ministry, and partnership is a commitment to missional living with the local body of believers. We call these men and women "partners" rather than "members," because we think that word more clearly describes the heart of the New Testament.[1]

The gospel certainly frees us to partner with God, but this is not a "partnership" between equals. The grace that makes it possible to know and partner with God is deeply humbling, and sets us up with the kind of posture we need to partner with one another. It shapes partnerships that are "built on relationships and trust, developed primarily by listening, conversation, and exploring possibilities."[2] Craig Ott and Gene Wilson relate partnership to Ecclesiastes' unbreakable threefold cord (4:9-12), noting that partnering extensively "helps to overcome the enormity of the task of world evangelization and permits good stewardship of the diverse resources needed for so great a task."[3] The benefits of locking arms seem endless. So why do we partner so little?

The biblical examples we've considered above not only model partnership for us, they also point to why it's so hard. Partnership always includes a laying down of personal rights, a bending to the benefit of others. John the Baptist decreased. Jesus exited. Paul gave God the credit. To partner well we sometimes have to lay down or share our logo. The real challenge of the 21st century is whether or not we will work together, partnering effectively with churches, agencies, and nationals.[4] Missiologist Eric Wright reasons that "the world hasn't been evangelized yet because Christians are attempting to do it independently, rather than together."[5] So maybe zeal isn't the issue, but wisdom. Busy people often try to resolve their busyness by becoming more tenaciously busy. Partnership and delegation take time and energy and a view toward the long-haul. Just as Bill Hybels has said that we are too busy *not* to pray, we are too busy *not to partner*.[6]

Sending churches partner to finish the race.

---

[1] The Austin Stone Community Church. *Partnership at The Austin Stone*. Retrieved from http://austinstone.org/connect/partnership.
[2] Pioneers USA. *Church Partners*. Retrieved from http://www.pioneers.org/Send/ChurchPartners.aspx.
[3] Craig Ott and Gene Wilson, *Global Church Planting: Biblical Principles and Best Practices for Multiplication* (Grand Rapids, MI: Baker Academic, 2011), 374.
[4] Michael Pocock, Gailyn Van Rheenen, and Douglas McConnell, *The Changing Face of World Missions: Engaging Contemporary Issues and Trends* (Grand Rapids, MI: Baker Academic, 2005), 271.
[5] Eric E. Wright, *A Practical Theology of Missions: Dispelling the Mystery, Recovering the Passion* (Leominster, UK: Day One Publications, 2010), 214.
[6] Bill Hybels, *Too Busy Not to Pray* (Downers Grove, IL: IVP Books, 2008).

with other churches or agencies

A Sending Church is a local community of Christ-followers who have made a covenant together to be prayerful, deliberate, and proactive in developing, commissioning, and sending their own members both locally and globally, often in partnership **with other churches or agencies**, and continuing to encourage, support, and advocate for them while making disciples cross-culturally.

Agencies

The Upstream Collective is all about churches reclaiming their identity as the leaders in mission. That's why we've been working through this definition. That's why we'll keep encouraging churches on mission. But what is our take on mission agencies? Where do they fit? Or do they fit at all? Let's start by taking a brief look at their storied past.

Unfortunately, the account doesn't begin with a clear scriptural model. Antioch in Acts 13 gives us the first basic glimpse of a sending church, but it would be a theological stretch in any direction to write an "agency" into the text. This continued throughout the first centuries of Christianity. The shift came, and came quickly, when the Roman Empire adopted Christianity as the state religion, forming monastic and sometimes military orders in advancing the faith. It became absurd to think individual churches were responsible for sending. During European imperialism mission was equated with colonization, and missionaries took their orders as much from the king as the church. The Protestant Reformation soon rocked the world, but did more to redefine the church-*gathered* than the church-*sent*. Leading up to the modern missions movement it was commonly accepted that churches *couldn't* and *shouldn't* send (insert Dr. Ryland's reply to William Carey: "Young man, sit down; when God is pleased to convert the heathen world, he will do it without your help or mine"[1]). When the passion of the modern missions movement converged with the idea that churches couldn't facilitate sending, mission agencies as we understand them today were born. By the 1920s, denominational agencies operated like American corporations and could function almost completely separate from churches— and the churches proudly outsourced their commission. Yet vast changes after World War II rearranged missions and mission agencies. The influential voices of Roland Allen and Lesslie Newbigin described the church as the missionary of God and begged for its centrality in mission.[2] Spurred on by globalization and denominational discontent, many churches began bypassing mission agencies to manage their own endeavors. Craig Ott and Stephen Strauss, who provided this helpful history, said that "from 1900 to 2000 the percentage of North American missionaries sent by mainline mission organizations dropped from 80 percent to only 6 percent."[3] In light of this swinging pendulum, we ask, has the (in)famous mission agency run its course?

No way! As Harry Boer writes, "The missionary society is, scripturally speaking, an abnormality. But it is a blessed abnormality."[4] Mission agencies have been uniquely used by God to initiate in mission at times when the church was simply unwilling to do so.[5] They remain a unique gift to the church, and what they bring to the table doesn't have to be reproduced by every local church. Eric Wright names some of the special characteristics of agencies: single-mindedness (aligned toward mission alone), specialization (professionalized in key aspects of mission), adaptability (rooted in the location of sent ones), simplicity (not subjected to ecclesiological processes), catholicity (united across different churches and traditions), spirituality (devoted to the spiritual vitality of sent ones), and accomplishment (structured to accomplish strategic goals).[6] Their sheer experience alone in the complex world of sending is enough to bring wise churches seeking advice and partnership. Does your church have the capacity to provide and manage the finances of all your sent ones? Can you develop strategy completely on your own? Do you know how to help evacuate sent ones after war breaks out? Yes, *we are saying that churches can do it all*, but reinventing the wheel may not always be the best use of time or resources. We're grateful for agencies. Wright even goes so far as to say that to "deny the validity of [them] is to seriously hamper the fulfillment of the missionary mandate."[7] We don't question their validity. We do, however, question their posture. To nuance Wright, the missionary mandate was given to the universal church expressed as local churches. Agencies, regardless of how well they have or continue to represent local churches, are not local churches. When agencies seek to take the lead in planting churches they showcase their pragmatic ecclesiology. And a pragmatic view of the church is a low view of the church. A healthy ecclesiology begins not with what can be done to make more churches, but what it is that makes churches who they are.[8]

For this kind of partnership to flourish as it should, there must be a clear presupposition: local churches "are the hub of the missions wheel, while mission agencies are spokes in the wheel helping churches extend their work."[9] Churches that haven't given up on agencies are looking to partner with agencies that haven't given up on churches. In talking with a pastor at a sending church this week, he mentioned four key elements in determining which agencies his church partners with:

- Church service – Are they devoted to empowering our church in mission?

- Relational accessibility – Are they going to consistently communicate with our church?

- Theological accord – Are they clinging to the same truths as our church?

- Strategic alignment – Are they fleshing out mission in similar ways as our church?

Inevitably, this reproof will be leveraged by some churches in an extreme pendulum shift. In youthful zeal they may seize the opportunity to commandeer their relationship with missions agencies, directing or bypassing them altogether. This would be just as unfortunate as our current situation—and just as unbiblical. Though the Scriptures offer no precedent for missions agencies, they do communicate a measure of autonomy among the apostolic teams during their missionary journeys. Make no mistake, Paul and his teams were profoundly attached to the local churches from which they were sent and supported, of whom they were an extension (Acts 14:26-28, Acts 20:36-38, Philippians 1:3-8). But many of their day-to-day and even strategic decisions appear to have come from their dependence on the Holy Spirit and one another rather than the micromanagement of the local church (Acts 16:6-10, Acts 21:10-14, Romans 15:17-22). Sending churches are responsible to lead their sent ones toward healthy ministries empowered by the Holy Spirit. In so doing they may choose to forego the wisdom and experience of mission agencies. Yet they will likely repeat many unnecessary mistakes and carry a weight that may at times be "too heavy [to] handle alone" (Exodus 18:18).

Patrick Johnstone sums it all up this way:
Possibly the most defective partnership is that between the mission agencies and local churches...it is the result of two centuries of mission agencies acting as if local churches were just a source of finance and people, and local churches acting irresponsibly in their roles of sending and supporting. The centrality of the local church in missions needs to be emphasized, and agencies must be more accountable to their supporting churches for their ministries and use of workers. However, both are vital components of the Church— and must work together. [10]

Healthy partnerships with mission agencies lead to so much more than could be accomplished separately. As sending churches lead their own people into mission, they are wise to take advantage of agencies' support.

Nationals

Opinions were hurtling across the room as a few dozen North American mission leaders gathered in a narrow Manhattan boardroom. The dialogue based on major global trends made for a warm and lively atmosphere. Then someone said it. "The U.S. is now receiving more missionaries than any country in the world. Shouldn't we stop *sending* so we can focus on *receiving*?" The ensuing silence, combined with more than a few dumbfounded facial expressions, left me on the edge of my seat. Finally, and almost simultaneously, there was a wave of polite yet assertive boos that obliterated the very thought of no longer sending the church on mission.

As thankful as I am to sit among leaders who understand and cultivate the sent identity of the church, I too have to admit that there are some really tough questions to answer about why and how we send. Yeah, the West is no longer the epicenter of Christianity as the church has exploded all over the world.[11] Churches in places we would never expect are sending thousands into the neighborhoods and nations.[12] How do we balance sending with being the largest recipient of those sent ones? Furthermore, would it be a better use of resources to send money instead of people? I mean, how many national pastors could we support with the $2.4 billion we spend each year just on sending short-term mission teams?[13]

The best way forward is rooted in global partnership. And this isn't simply because "the task is far too big for any one group to manage on its own."[14] Sending was never meant to be monopolized. Bill Taylor writes,

Surely there is some relationship between partnership in mission and the prayer of our Lord in John 17:11, 21-13. Four times our Lord prayed that

111

ultimately God would enable us to demonstrate a marvelous unity that will make Christ Himself visible to the world.[15]

We catch a glimpse of this kind of partnership in Paul's relationship with the church in Rome. Paul's posture of servanthood[16] is apparent from the very beginning of his letter to the Roman Christians: "For I long to see you, that I may impart to you some spiritual gift to strengthen you" (1:11). Now before we use this verse to justify our paternal tendencies toward locals in the neighborhood and nationals around the world, as though we have everything to give and they have nothing to offer, let's consider how Paul completes the sentence: "that is, that we may be mutually encouraged by each other's faith, both yours and mine." Partnership begins with the conviction that both groups bring value to the table. They need each other. Nepali pastors don't just need Western churches to come and teach about church administration. Western churches need Nepali pastors to teach them—not only what we think we need—but what *they* discern are *our* shortcomings.

This means redefining our sense of partnership altogether. Ron Blue says that "although we in North America talk much about *partnership,* in reality we're talking about *sponsorship.*"[17] National partners have traditionally been those we "help" in some way. But sending churches understand the difference between a sponsor and a partner. Paul did, and showcases it in Romans 15:24, "I hope to see you in passing as I go to Spain, and to be helped on my journey there by you, once I have enjoyed your company for a while." He hoped to team up with the Romans in advancing the gospel to Spain. Between himself and them he naturally expected mutual submission with mutual encouragement for mutual mission. That's partnership.

Alas, if it only played out that easily! Tension often begins as soon as money is involved—more specifically, when it's requested or relinquished or refused. Much financial hesitancy and frustration comes directly from cultural differences.[18] How do you choose a trustworthy partner? How do they choose you? How do you keep accountability from feeling like colonialism? What is appropriate to expect in return? It all takes cultural intelligence.[19]

And to gain cultural intelligence, relationship is required. But "too often, Western Christians forget that demonstrating love in the context of relationships is the very essence of Christian living."[20] We're eager to make them a product or project. Where might we gain a better understanding of relationship? From those of the global church themselves, whose lives often center on relationship. An African church leader advises that we must be like "the two friends on the road to Emmaus...What we need to seek out are those

113

whom the Lord may want us to travel with [while] following him."[21]

Global partnerships are "profound blessings,"[22] and sending churches walk their paths.

Churches

The first time I served on a church staff the pastor took me with him to a state denominational meeting of church leaders. As a college student the culture was quite foreign. I picked up pretty quick, however, that the nicer your suit, the larger your entourage, and the greater number of people who lined up to nervously shake your hand, the more important you were. But nothing prepared me for the gathering in which a speaker began divvying out certificates, plaques, and trophies to pastors for their churches' "performance" in mission. We stood at the end to praise God for how we had stirred "up one another on to love and good deeds" (Hebrews 10:24), but it all sniffed to me more like every man for himself, a bit more capitalist than Christian.

Now capitalism certainly does a remarkably good job of keeping us motivated by competition. But is that how God compels churches into his mission together? Given, the Scriptures do speak of us outdoing one another, but in "showing honor" (Romans 12:10), not in showing off. Paul also said of false teachers that "when they measure

114

themselves by one another and compare themselves with one another, they are without understanding" (2 Corinthians 10:12). When our churches celebrate what they've individually done without grieving and striving together for what is still undone, aren't we missing the point? If what a church is doing "downplays teamwork...it betrays the model left by the Master."[23]

Throughout the New Testament we see glimpses of partnership between churches in a variety of ways. There's collaboration in doctrine (Jerusalem Council, Acts 15), mercy (Macedonian collection, 2 Corinthians 8), church planting (Ephesus, Acts 19), and missionary care (Gaius, 3 John) just to name a few. Perhaps more than the models, however, the principles of the Scriptures apply to church partnerships. Almost everything that has been described thus far, and will be described about an individual sending church, may also be applied to churches partnering together.

Partnerships "facilitate the planting of new kingdom communities by strategically bringing together complementary gifts and resources."[24] Like the old cartoon, *Captain Planet*, they synergize by combining what each church uniquely brings to the table for the sake of a greater impact in mission. But this subtly implies that awkward confession again: *we need each other*. Why would we ever approach the overwhelming task of local and global mission alone?[25] The indictment of the gospel echoes similarly on the subject of church partnerships: we are desperately needy. Every church has what it takes to do something, but no church alone has what it takes to do everything.

One modern attempt at church partnership was missions societies. The idea was that a church seeking to send cross-culturally would compel other churches nearby to buy into the mission and missionaries—literally and figuratively. Together, they would send them. Southern Baptists nuanced this concept with the inauguration of the Southern Baptist Convention, and nuanced it once more with the Cooperative Program, a way for churches to channel a percentage of their giving into one pool. This was done "for the purpose of organizing a practical plan on which the energies of the whole Baptist denomination may be elicited, combined and directed in one sacred effort for sending the word of life to idolatrous lands."[26] And it has been a remarkable convergence of resources. But churches have more to offer one another than money.

And the way churches offer those resources can look different. Here are a few examples:

- A consortium of interdenominational churches in the greater Milwaukee area partner together to support work in Indonesia.[27]

- Fairhaven Church in Dayton, Ohio started both a multi-national church network (a collaboration between six churches, one on each continent) and missions fellowship among churches in their city.[28]

- Lifepoint Church in Smyrna, Tennessee enjoyed an unofficial partnership with another US church they happened to meet who were seeking to do similar work in Brussels, Belgium.[29]

- Leaders at SBC Virginia set up the Acts 1:8 Network, intentionally connecting churches who are reaching out to the same affinities.[30]

Even Upstream itself is a *collective* of churches. Despite their imperfections, these kinds of partnerships can make it "possible to mobilize a variety of groups and individuals to participate in a strategy to influence a city or even the globe."[31] That's why there's all the fuss about sending church roundtables and cohorts and conferences and resources. Churches need one another in figuring this stuff out. And as they do, they can accomplish things like sending inter-church teams, sharing the load of missionary care, co-funding projects and personnel, learning from best and worst practices, encouraging one another through setbacks, etc.

However, since partnerships are essentially relationships, not all of them will work out.[32] Like

Paul and Barnabas, God may sovereignly use sharp differences to expand his mission even more broadly. Yet that will not make them any less painful or cumbersome to walk through. As pastor and missionary Kyle Goen has written, partnership "isn't easy. There is definitive give-and-take. But, the gospel of Jesus is well worth the risk."[33]

And the sprawling global commission of Jesus demands it.[34] Sending churches make a sending church.

[1] Clifford G. Howell, *The Advanced Guard of Missions* (Mountain View, CA: Pacific Press Publishing, 1912).

[2] Roland Allen, *The Spontaneous Expansion of the Church: And the Causes That Hinder It* (Eugene, OR: Wifp and Stock Publishers, 1962); Lesslie Newbigin, *The Open Secret: An Introduction to the Theology of Mission* (Grand Rapids, MI: Eerdmans, 1995).

[3] Craig Ott, Stephen J. Strauss, and Timothy C. Tennent, *Encountering Theology of Missions: Biblical Foundations, Historical Developments, and Contemporary Issues* (Grand Rapids, MI: Baker Academic, 2010), 202-208.

[4] Ibid., 208.

[5] Paul A. Beals, *A People for His Name: A Church-Based Missions Strategy* (Pasadena, CA: William Carey Library, 2013), 137.

[6] Eric E. Wright, *A Practical Theology of Missions: Dispelling the Mystery, Recovering the Passion* (Leominster, UK: Day One Publications, 2010), 222.

[7] Ibid., 222.

[8] Gregg R. Allison, *Sojourners and Strangers: The Doctrine of the Church* (Wheaton, IL: Crossway, 2012), 123-160.

[9] Beals, *People*, 133.

[10] Patrick Johnstone, *The Future of the Global Church: History, Trends, and Possibilities* (Downers Grove, IL: IVP Books, 2011), 234.

[11] Miriam Adeney, *Kingdom Without Borders: The Untold Story of Global Christianity* (Downers Grove, IL: IVP Books, 2009).

[12] Melissa Steffan. (25 July 2013). *The Surprising Countries Most Missionaries are Sent From and Go To.* Retrieved from http://www.christianitytoday.com/gleanings/2013/july/missionaries-countries-sent-received-csgc-gordon-conwell.html?paging=off.

[13] Darren Carlson. (10 June 2012). *Celebrating the Short-Term Missions Boom.* Retrieved from http://www.thegospelcoalition.org/article/celebrating-the-short-term-missions-boom/.

[14] Paul Borthwick, *Western Christians in Global Mission: What's the Role of the North American Church?* (Downers Grove, IL: IVP Books, 2012), 152.

[15] Ralph D. Winter, *Perspectives on the World Christian Movement: A Reader, Third Ed* (Pasadena, CA: William Carey Library, 1999), 752; see Bill Taylor's chapter, "Lessons of Partnership".

[16] Duane Elmer, *Cross-Cultural Servanthood: Serving the World in Christlike Humility* (Downers Grove, IL: IVP Books, 2006); this is perhaps the best resource on servanthood as it relates to mission.

[17] Borthwick, *Western*, 150; quote is taken from Ron Blue.

[18] Mary T. Lederleitner, *Cross-Cultural Partnership: Navigating the Complexities of Money and Mission* (Downers Grove, IL: IVP Books, 2010).

[19] David A. Livermore, *Cultural Intelligence: Improving Your CQ to Engage Our Multicultural World* (Grand Rapids, MI: Baker Academic, 2009).

[20] Wright, *Theology*, 215.

[21] Borthwick, *Western*, 159; quote is taken from Zac Niringiye.

[22] Winter, *Perspectives*, 747; see Larry Keyes' chapter, "A Global Harvest Force".

[23] Wright, *Theology*, 208.

[24] Craig Ott and Gene Wilson, *Global Church Planting: Biblical Principles and Best Practices for Multiplication* (Grand Rapids, MI: Baker Academic, 2011), 373.

[25] Mike Barnett, Ed., *Discovering the Mission of God: Best Missional Practices for the 21st Century* (Downers Grove, IL: IVP Academic, 2012), 323-338; see J. Scott Holste's chapter, "Finishing the Task".

[26] Jerry Rankin, *To the Ends of the Earth: Churches Fulfilling the Great Commission* (Richmond, VA: International Mission Board, 2005), 120; quote is taken from John T. Christian.

[27] Ott and Wilson, *Global*, 377.

[28] Tom Telford, *Today's All-Star Missions Churches: Strategies to Help Your Church Get Into the Game* (Grand Rapids, MI: Baker, 2001), 91-92.

[29] Kyle Goen. (21 July 2014). *with other churches or agencies, part 3.* Retrieved from http://theupstreamcollective.org/2014/07/21/with-other-churches-or-agencies-part-3/.

[30] SBC of Virginia. (13 December 2011). *About the Acts 1:8 Network.* Retrieved from http://www.sbcv.org/articles/detail/about_the_acts_18_network.

[31] Michael Pocock, Gailyn Van Rheenen, and Douglas McConnell, *The Changing Face of World Missions: Engaging Contemporary Issues and Trends* (Grand Rapids, MI: Baker Academic, 2005), 261-262.

[32] Ott and Wilson, *Global*, 382.

[33] Goen, *with other churches or agencies, part 3,*

[34] Johnstone, *Future*, 234.

and continuing to

A Sending Church is a local community of Christ-followers who have made a covenant together to be prayerful, deliberate, and proactive in developing, commissioning, and sending their own members both locally and globally, often in partnership with other churches or agencies, **and continuing to** encourage, support, and advocate for them while making disciples cross-culturally.

The Challenge For Missionaries

Ebola. Who's ready to get *that*?

Missionaries to Liberia, Kent Brantly and Nancy Writebol, certainly weren't.[1] And odds are their home churches weren't either. Sure, everyone considers the inherit dangers of moving into cross-cultural neighborhoods and nations, especially in the majority world. But it's hard to plan for what *could happen* in the flurry of demands that *are happening*.

So why try?

Because it's part of being a sending church. How to shepherd our Kent Brantlys and Nancy Writebols—or more commonly, our furloughing, transitioning, and

121

retiring sent ones—*is* our concern. Most everything that we've discussed in the definition thus far has focused on two phases: before missionaries are sent and while they're on the field. But there's an entire third phase to consider: when sent ones return.

Unfortunately, this crucial last phase is the ugly duckling of the sending process. As one missions pastor said recently, "When you send out troops, they're going to come back wounded." On multiple occasions Paul describes the harrowing plight of being on the forefront of advancing the gospel (Romans 8: 35-39, 1 Corinthians 4:8-13, 2 Corinthians 11:23-29). Even from his conversion we see God's sobering intention for him: "For I will show him how much he must suffer for the sake of my name" (Acts 9:16). Now while we wouldn't describe Paul's sufferings as regulatory for all sent ones, they do represent the general nature of the business. Being sent doesn't always mean signing up for death, but a series of small deaths. Kelly O'Donnell writes,

From the day one enters the process of becoming a missionary, spiritual, emotional, interpersonal, and physical stresses begin to multiply, and these stresses usually continue unabated throughout one's career.[2]

Sarah Hay points to a study that shows "40% of aid workers develop a psychological disorder (such as depression) while on the field or shortly after returning home."[3] And Justin Long notes that around 20% of first-term missionaries don't make it, though the stat is debated to be as high as 75%.[4]

The glories of battle that carried thousands of young Americans into the Civil War faded with horrific finality in infamous field hospitals. Tending the wounded was a hard sell. And it still is. Yet churches, like the missionaries they send to preach and heal, can wade into brokenness with the confidence and hope that only the gospel provides. They can offer ongoing encouragement, support, and advocacy during the unique challenges sent ones face each time they return for the following reasons.

Furlough

Furloughs can be sacred times for sent ones. They are intended to provide the cultural distance to rest, renew contact with the church and family, raise funds, recruit workers, report the ministry, reintroduce children to their homeland, and refresh training.[5] Yet they sometimes can be just the opposite thanks to missionary kryptonite—reentry. After all the adjustments of language and culture, reentering one's home culture "can cause as much or more stress than going to the field."[6] Marion Knell uses the analogy of a spaceship reentering earth's atmosphere to parallel reentry—but says it's ultimately more like being an alien on a flying saucer.[7] And it's the *most* difficult for children (or

TCKs—third culture kids) because reentry is more like entry, as they've often only known life elsewhere.[8]

Transition

Transition is a catch-all for any reason that a sent one returns. This category could also be called "failure," not because returning sent ones are failures, but because regardless of their circumstance they are often undeservedly viewed as such. The church can easily exalt missionaries as heroes, and thus struggle to have a category for them when they return "prematurely". Common reasons for missionary attrition include lack of financial support, conflict, marriage for singles, culture shock, expulsion, persecution, lack of fruit, emotional trauma, a sense of God's leadership, moral failure, loss of vision, lack of care, physical illness, family dilemmas, educational needs, and change of assignment.[9] As you can imagine, an entire host of hardships can accompany the internal and external disappointment of transitioning home.

Retirement

Retirement "is as important a stage in missionary life as the other stages," and yet is no less challenging.[10] John Piper has famously challenged cultural retirement ease in favor of leveraging one's golden years for God's glory.[11] Right on. But that doesn't mean that missionaries should never relinquish their posts. Everyone must pass the baton at some point. Yet bidding farewell to the field can be as hard for a sent one as giving up the car keys for an ailing parent. It's common for their most severe identity crisis to occur in the midst of permanent reentry. And the grief of final goodbyes can be overwhelming, not to mention looming financial and health concerns.

The challenges of the third phase of the sending process are heavy indeed. But take heart! There's so much that sending churches can do about it.

The Opportunity for Churches

Now it would be rather American of us to make the sending process into a packaged deal. *For only three easy payments (plus shipping and handling) you can be developed, sent, and received back without a scratch!* That would be consumerism on mission. And there's not much room for consumerism in Paul when he speaks of being satisfied with plentiful support *or* lacking support (Philippians 4:10-13). Nor is there much among Chinese missionaries in Damascus, Syria or church planters in Ferguson, Missouri.[12] No, sending churches don't *prevent* all the suffering of their sent ones, but they do help *relieve* some of it.

How do they do that? Well, the short answer is they *continue* to do the things we've yet to discuss in the sending church definition (encourage, support, and advocate) as their sent ones return for furlough, transition, and retirement. But let's flesh that out a bit.

Neal Pirolo has identified a model for missionary care in Barnabas and Paul's return from their first journey. Acts 14:26-28 and 15:35 describe the arrival back at Antioch, their sending church. As part of this reentry, Barnabas and Paul did five things: completed their assignment, returned to their sending church, shared life with them for a long time, reported all that God had done, and became active in the church's local mission again.[13] If these are the basic biblical steps that returning sent ones should walk through, then what do sending churches do to help facilitate those steps?

Planning

First, they think ahead. They don't wait until their sent ones arrive back home to take action. They're not necessarily ready for everything, but try to make a basic plan unique to their church. Here's some of the questions they've been thinking through: Who will greet the missionaries at the airport? How will we help them find a place to live? What are our expectations for where they'll go to church (don't assume—many missionaries choose to live near family rather than their sending church)? How will we provide opportunities for them to report to the church and celebrate what God has done? How will we debrief them? What can we do to support them financially during this season? What are our sent ones' expectations of us? What will we do if they need counseling? What if they're ill? How do we want them to become active in the church's local mission again? How can we love their children well? What's our long-term commitment to their assimilation realistically look like? And how will we involve the entire church so we don't die trying to do it ourselves?

Presence

Sending churches understand that no amount of logistical support can replace their genuine presence. They ask good questions and listen, which puts them well on their way to debriefing their missionaries. Debriefing literally means "talking through an experience after it has taken place."[14] For sent ones it should involve questions related to their soul, ministry, and any traumatic experiences during their service.[15] And active listening involves much more than resisting the urge to check your phone. Many missionaries are "afraid of losing support if they share some of their more difficult struggles."[16] Can they be *really* honest with you? The level of discomfort you have when they pour out their hearts points directly to the height of the missionary pedestal your church has built. A culture of vulnerability fashioned by grace is crucial to the health of returning missionaries (not to mention everyone else!).

Finally, sending churches provide for their returning sent ones in proportion to what they've been given (2 Corinthians 8:8-15) and in correlation with the sacrifice the sent ones have made (3 John: 5-8). Just as they articulate to all church members, they give not reluctantly or under compulsion, but cheerfully. They have decided what the church will be responsible for and what the missionaries will be responsible for. Then they have articulated it to those already on the field and to those still in their development process. False expectations murder relationships. They contribute something to their housing and transportation, even if it's just a full pantry and a ride to Carmax. Whether or not they can pay for it, sending churches do well to provide guidance toward good counseling. One missions pastors sends all his returning missionaries to at least one session with a local Christian counselor for what he calls a "tune-up". It's especially helpful to make a game plan for leading retiring missionaries through financial and identity crises. The amount of time a missionary served overseas is often comparable to the time it takes them to fully readjust to the states. For retiring ones, they may never readjust. Will your church be indifferent, judgmental, or full of grace and truth?

For all the hardships missionaries return with, they also come bearing gifts for the church. Their experience, wisdom, passion—even their wounds—

can build up the body of Christ. Veteran missionary Thomas Hale says that returning "isn't all 'getting'... the greater part is giving, especially to churches at home."[17] Most returning missionaries desperately need clearly defined boundaries and onramps for becoming active in the church's local mission again. It's easy for them to be either overwhelmed or underutilized. Church leaders who shepherd them wisely will watch both the sent and the senders benefit.

One church said recently, "We are about ten years behind the sending church paradigm." Considering this chapter a checklist could certainly make you feel that way. Instead, dream big and start small. It will mean the world your sent ones.

[1] Kate Taylor. (8 August 2014). *Indy Native with Ebola Releases Statement*. Retrieved from http://wishtv.com/2014/08/08/indy-native-with-ebola-releases-statement/; Associated Press. (5 August 2014). *American Missionary with Ebola En Route to US*. Retrieved from http://nypost.com/2014/08/05/american-missionary-infected-with-ebola-en-route-to-us/.

[2] Kelly O'Donnell, *Missionary Care: Counting the Cost for World Evangelization* (Elizabethton, TN: William Carey Library, 1999), 47.

[3] Rob Hay, Valerie Lim, Detlef Blocher, Jaap Ketelaar, and Sarah Hay, *Worth Keeping: Global Perspectives on Best Practice in Missionary Retention* (Elizabethton, TN: William Carey Library, 2013), 386.

[4] Justin Long. (6 July 2011). *75% Leave the Field in the First 3 Years, Never Return? It's a Myth—Sort Of*. Retrieved from http://www.justinlong.org/2011/07/75-leave-the-field-in-the-first-3-years-never-return-its-a-myth-sort-of/.

[5] Thomas Hale, *On Being a Missionary* (Elizabethton, TN: William Carey Library, 2012), 392.

[6] O'Donnell, *Missionary*, 310.

[7] Marion Knell, *Burn-Up or Splash Down: Surviving the Culture Shock of Re-Entry* (Downers Grove, IL: IVP Books, 2007), 4.

[8] David C. Pollock and Ruth E. Van Reken, *Third Culture Kids: Growing Up Among Worlds* (Boston, MA: Nicholas Brealey Publishing, 2009), 226.

[9] William Taylor, *Too Valuable to Lose: Exploring the Causes and Cures of Missionary Attrition* (Elizabethton, TN: William Carey Library, 1997).

[10] O'Donnell, *Missionary*, 312.

[11] John Piper. (13 February 2011). *Don't Waste Your Retirement*. Retrieved from https://www.youtube.com/watch?v=mSl_SCQkaYg.

[12] Back to Jerusalem. (22 August 2013). *BTJ Missionaries in Syria*. Retrieved from https://backtojerusalem.com/v3/2013/08/btj-missionaries-in-syria/; Tobin Perry. (15 August 2014). *St. Louis Planters Organize Ferguson Cleanup*. Retrieved from http://www.namb.net/nambblogSt.Louis.aspx?id=12884911351&blogid=8590116839.

[13] Neal Pirolo, *The Reentry Team: Caring for Your Returning Missionaries* (San Diego, CA: Emmaus Road International, 2000), 24.

[14] Hay, *Worth*, 385.

[15] O'Donnell, *Missionary*.

[16] Sue Eenigenburg and Robynn Bliss, *Expectations and Burnout: Women Surviving the Great Commission* (Elizabethton, TN: William Carey Library, 2010), 98.

[17] Hale, *Being*, 394.

encourage

> A Sending Church is a local community of Christ-followers who have made a covenant together to be prayerful, deliberate, and proactive in developing, commissioning, and sending their own members both locally and globally, often in partnership with other churches or agencies, and continuing to **encourage**, support, and advocate for them while making disciples cross-culturally.

My home [church] said they would write to me and pray for me. I wrote to them faithfully about every five weeks...I received a form letter once a year from them telling me what they were doing (yes, I was even listed as one of their 'accomplishments'!), but they never once asked me how I was doing...I felt they didn't care.[1]

Many similar words have bled across the journal pages of those sent far from their local church, the family who nursed and nourished them as they wrestled with a missional dream, the people who promised to hold the rope and never let go. A sending church could commit no less crime than pouring all its energies into development only to neglect ongoing support. Perhaps nothing could set up a sent one for failure more than the expectations that they will be loved and remembered if, in fact, they won't be. Let's be clear, sending doesn't end once the commissioning is done.

There is one exception, however. In Gethsemane Jesus mourned on the precipice of completing his mission. It's what he'd been sent to do, what he longed to finish. So why the bloody sweat?[2] Because he was to be forsaken. His bros would scatter. The rope that the Father had held was to be completely severed and he would finish alone. The wonder of our Savior is that he *did* finish the mission, abandonment and all. Yet his example here is *descriptive* of the gospel that saves us, not *prescriptive* for the life that we must somehow figure out how to live. Only Jesus could face a cross without the encouragement of others.

Unfortunately, many have had to brave tough neighborhoods and nations without their church pouring courage into them through words and actions. Neal Pirolo reminds us that when "Paul was determined to go to Jerusalem, throngs of people… tried to dissuade him."[3] Supporting churches among the pages of missions history are few and far between. And yet "mission is not something somebody else does who is far away and whom we hardly know. Mission is something we do—we all do —together."[4] The idea of goers and senders is not a new one, but it's never been a widely popular one.[5] However, the embracing of mission by the entire church body is the best way for it to move forward. And nowhere it is more crucial than in the ongoing support of those sent out. "I have no doubt," says Eric Wright poignantly, "that some missionary casualties could have been avoided by paying more attention to missionary care."[6]

Sending is a commitment to the long haul care of those sent out. And encouragement "is the foundation of the sending process...it is as much an attitude that your cross-cultural worker will sense as it is an action you can do."[7] It's the "quality time" of good communication.[8] It's Skype calls and emails and notes where you can "speak the truth in love... making the body grow so that it builds itself up in love" (Ephesians 4:15-16). It's being able to have honest conversations where you find out how to help and how to pray. And it's developing a church culture where more than a handful of people are doing this. That means it must be a priority to the senior pastor.[9]

But the benefit is not solely for the sent ones. "No local church can go without the encouragement and nourishment that will come to it by sending out its best people."[10] As we see in the life of Paul, the lives and ministries of global sent ones can and should be leveraged in encouraging the senders to fulfill their local mission. That's why *Tradecraft* was written, so that the church would be empowered with missionary ninja skills for every member in their daily context.[11] But think of the combined gain of ongoing mutual encouragement from sent ones, often some of your best leaders. Keep them before your people, and wide-eyed children will be pointed to the worth of Jesus, waylaid church members will be reminded of the powerful God in *their* midst too, and weary pastors will marvel at God's gracious extension of their ministry. There is rich return awaiting the sending church that keeps its hands on the rope.

[1] Neal Pirolo, *Serving as Senders* (San Diego, CA: Emmaus Road International, 1991), 119-121.

[2] H. R. Jerajani, Bhagyashri Jaju, M. M. Phiske, and Nitin Lade. (July-September 2009). *Hematohidrosis: A Rare Clinical Phenomenon.* Retrieved from http://www.ncbi.nlm.nih.gov/pmc/articles/PMC2810702/.

[3] Neal Pirolo, *Serving as Senders - Today* (San Diego, CA: Emmaus Road International, 2012), 33.

[4] George Miley, *Loving the Church, Blessing the Nations: Pursuing the Role of Local Churches in Global Mission* (Downers Grove, IL: IVP Books, 2005), 192.

[5] John Piper. (24 June 2011). *Goers, Senders, and the Disobedient.* Retrieved from http://www.desiringgod.org/interviews/goers-senders-and-the-disobedient.

[6] Eric E. Wright, *A Practical Theology of Missions: Dispelling the Mystery, Recovering the Passion* (Leominster, UK: Day One Publications, 2010), 232.

[7] Pirolo, *Serving*, 40.

[8] Paul A. Beals, *A People for His Name: A Church-Based Missions Strategy* (Pasadena, CA: William Carey Library, 2013), 113.

[9] Ibid., 78.

[10] John Piper. (25 November 1991). *Soundbites from the Battlefield.* Retrieved from http://www.desiringgod.org/articles/soundbites-from-the-battlefield; quote is taken from David Penman.

[11] Larry E. McCrary, Caleb Crider, Wade Stephens, and Rodney Calfee, *Tradecraft: For the Church on Mission* (Portland, OR: Urban Loft Publishers, 2013).

support

A Sending Church is a local community of Christ-followers who have made a covenant together to be prayerful, deliberate, and proactive in developing, commissioning, and sending their own members both locally and globally, often in partnership with other churches or agencies, and continuing to encourage, **support**, and advocate for them while making disciples cross-culturally.

Beloved, it is a faithful thing you do in all your efforts for these brothers, strangers as they are, who testified to your love before the church. You will do well to send them on their journey in a manner worthy of God. For they have gone out for the sake of the name, accepting nothing from the Gentiles. Therefore we ought to support people like these, that we may be fellow workers for the truth. (3 John: 5-8)

Who would've thought that such significant words for the sending church would come from such a tiny letter! In a brief correspondence with his friend, Gaius, the apostle John rejoiced that he was "walking in the truth" (v. 3). This was evidenced in large part by Gaius' *working* for the truth. How was Gaius working for the truth? By *supporting* those sent out from the church to proclaim the truth. He was practically making the mission possible.

The church cannot be the church without sending, and sending cannot happen without support. Expert in missionary care, Kelly O'Donnell, writes, "It is imperative that the local church play a larger role in world missions, particularly in the care and development of missionaries that they send out."[1] He even places support on par with key missions aspects, such as strategy and contextualization.[2] But what exactly is support? Is it just money?

Christoph Stenschke says that support reflected in the New Testament is the financial maintenance of missionaries, the provision of co-laborers, and prayer for the workers and the work.[3] Neal Pirolo adds logistics to the list.[4] And Eric Wright includes accountability.[5] Let's take a look at each one.

Finances

According to professor Craig Blomberg, Gaius' support of the sent ones referred to in 3 John probably included not only "bed and board, [but also] often donated funds as well [pay] for past or future travel expenses."[6] Gaius had put his money where his mouth was. In Paul we see examples of both ongoing support from the church (Romans 15:24, 1 Corinthians 9:14, Titus 3:13) as well as one-time gifts to advance the mission (Romans

15:26, 2 Corinthians 8-9, Philippians 4:18). John Stott applies this in his commentary on John's epistles by affirming that "Christians should finance Christian enterprises...there are many good causes which we *may* support; but we *must* support our brothers and sisters whom the world does not support."[7]

Realistically, however, most churches cannot fully support every missionary whom they send out. Even in light of God's abundant provision and believers' sacrificial generosity, churches have limited resources to steward. That's why pastor David Horner says that his church "soon realized that if [they] were going to reach the nations beyond [their] borders, [they] needed a strategic plan for how [their] dollars would be invested."[8]

Support is firstly financial, and it must be strategic to have the greatest impact.

Co-laborers

It only takes a skimming of the book of Acts to see that Paul rolled with an entourage. As reflected in the Trinity, community and mission go hand in hand. So Paul regularly sought from the church his most critical missional resource: co-laborers. He took Silas with him in Acts 15:40, commanded Timothy to come to him ASAP in Acts 17:15, and even beckoned for formerly disappointing John Mark in 2 Timothy 4:11.

Likewise, today the sending church eagerly seeks to outfit its sent ones with co-laborers through short-term teams, mid-term apprentices, and long-term partners.

Prayer

Jason Mandryk , author of *Operation World: The Definitive Prayer Guide to Every Nation*, says that "missions and prayer for the world should be at the heart of every [church]."[9] Paul certainly held this conviction long before us, as he consistently asked churches for prayer in his letters to them (Ephesians 6:19, 1 Timothy 2:1, 2 Thessalonians 3:1). Sending churches are praying churches. According to Tom Telford's study of all-star missions churches, this form of support can and should involve the entire church.[10]

Logistics & Accountability

"Nobody can handle everything!" is Pirolo's tagline for the critical role of logistical support.[11] Thriving cross-culturally involves a host of finely-detailed challenges. We see snippets of this in Paul's life, such as his request for "the cloak I left with Carpus at Troas and the books, but especially the parchments"[12]. The church has the capacity to lend a hand, allowing sent ones more freedom to focus on the work. Closely related is the concept of accountability. Wright notes that sent ones, like all of

us, need accountability to remain focused and doctrinally sound. "Churches should not feel they are intruding by lovingly monitoring their missionaries' work."[13] It's actually a *support*.

And that's the very thing sending churches are eager to do.

[1] Kelly O'Donnell, *Missionary Care: Counting the Cost for World Evangelization* (Elizabethton, TN: William Carey Library, 1999), 299.
[2] Ibid., xiii.
[3] Robert L. Plummer and John Mark Terry, *Paul's Missionary Methods: In His Time and Ours* (Downers Grove, IL: IVP Academic, 2012), 80; see Christoph Stenchke's chapter, "Paul's Mission as the Mission of the Church"; quote is taken from John P. Dickson.
[4] Neal Pirolo, *Serving as Senders: Today* (San Diego, CA: Emmaus Road International, 2012), 54.
[5] Eric E. Wright, *A Practical Theology of Missions: Dispelling the Mystery, Recovering the Passion* (Leominster, UK: Day One Publications, 2010), 230.
[6] Craig L. Blomberg, *From Pentecost to Patmos: An Introduction to Acts through Revelation* (Nashville, TN: B&H Academic, 2006), 503.
[7] John R. W. Stott, *The Epistles of John* (Grand Rapids, MI: Eerdmans, 1988), 227.
[8] David Horner, *When Missions Shapes the Mission: You and Your Church Can Reach the World* (Nashville, TN: B&H Academic, 2011), 170.
[9] Jason Mandryk, *Operation World: The Definitive Prayer Guide to Every Nation* (Downers Grove, IL: IVP Books, 2010), xxiii.
[10] Tom Telford, *Today's All-Star Missions Churches: Strategies to Help Your Church Get Into the Game* (Grand Rapids, MI: Baker, 2001), 28.
[11] Pirolo, *Serving*, 54.
[12] 2 Timothy 4:13, NIV.
[13] Wright, *Theology*, 232.

advocate for them

A Sending Church is a local community of Christ-
followers who have made a covenant together to be
prayerful, deliberate, and proactive in developing,
commissioning, and sending their own members
both locally and globally, often in partnership with
other churches or agencies, and continuing to
encourage, support, and **advocate for them** while
making disciples cross-culturally.

So ongoing missionary care is a big deal. The point
has been made. No one's saying that churches
shouldn't support their sent ones. But what we may
be thinking in the awkward silence is how does this
realistically work? How does a culture that moves at
the speed of light keep up with sent ones who are
out of sight and out of mind? Life goes on. Shoot,
ministry goes on. Missionary care seems like a novel
idea that overloaded pastors can retweet but not
repeat. But it's doable. And here's why.

The Church Advocate

Advocacy is an expression of God. The Scriptures
regularly stress God as advocate, fully pictured in all
three Persons: the Father (Deuteronomy 10:18,
Psalm 68:5), the Son (1 John 2:1, Romans 8:34,
Hebrews 7:25), and the Spirit (John 14:26, Romans
8:27). As a people of the Triune God, the church

gets advocacy. They are advocated for in ways they cannot yet fully fathom, and they're to bear the same joyous ministry of advocacy. This means the church advocates for God to people (2 Corinthians 5:18-20) and advocates for people to God (Genesis 18:22-33, Colossians 4:3, James 5:16). We cannot fail to understand advocacy unless we fail to understand our identity in Christ.

The Advocate Church

The other reason why pastors can lead their churches into missionary support without neglecting other important responsibilities is also rooted in the Trinity. The Father, Son, and Spirit are a community of advocacy. Their championing of one another teaches the church to do the same —advocating for one another to one another. This is especially true for those serving and suffering for the advance of the gospel cross-culturally (1 Thessalonians 3:6, 1 Timothy 5:17, 3 John: 6). Pastors who give their churches a vision of God can also give their churches a vision for selflessly and sacrificially cheering one another on for the sake of the gospel.

Imagine your church not only sending members out, but also commissioning advocate teams to support them. These teams take the lead in staying in contact, praying with insight, and sending needed resources. And then they pound the table among the church, keeping the sent ones' needs before everyone. Here are a few churches who are seeking to do this well:

Bethlehem Baptist Church – Under the leadership of John Piper, Bethlehem became one of the most influential sending churches in North America. They approach missionary care through what they call "Barnabas Support Teams,""small group[s] of committed people who come together to care for a particular global partner in a variety of ways, striving to help meet their physical, emotional and spiritual needs."[1]

The Austin Stone Community Church – Using a similar model, Austin Stone provides what they call "Advocate Teams". These teams are "group[s] of 6-12 individuals who take the responsibility to coordinate [the] church's support and encouragement of one of [their missionaries]...and to serve as their representatives to the Austin Stone church body. The team is [their] primary link between the Goer and the rest of [their] church."[2]

Sojourn Community Church – As part of their development process Sojourn puts the responsibility on missionary candidates to establish their own "Advocate Teams" from church members with whom they've shared life deeply. For the benefit of both the sent ones and the entire church body, candidates are also expected to recruit a few community groups to "adopt" them.[3]

College Park Church – College Park utilizes "Barnabas Teams" as their missionaries' "spiritual and emotional lifeline". They also channel anyone interested in missions to join Barnabas Team gatherings for prayer. This is the basic entry point of commitment to global missions for anyone in the church.[4]

Hershey Evangelical Free Church – Hershey has found that the more they improve their advocacy, the more church members come forward to be sent.[5]

Grace Covenant Church – Grace encourages families to serve on "Advocate Teams" who don't know the sent ones well so that it involves more of the church.[6]

An advocate team is just as important to today's sent ones as it was to the apostle Paul.[7] Thomas Sanchez at Grace Covenant says that "each local sending church can, and should, offer this kind of 'family' that is rarely provided by missions agencies."[8] If the kind of care we've addressed over the last few chapters is consistently making its way from the church to the sent ones, they may not only survive, but thrive in their life and ministry.

Yet the biggest impact may not be quite where we would expect. Those who don't go cross-culturally are just as commissioned to participate in the mission of God. What do you think might happen to your church as members are immersed in advocacy—praying and experiencing answers, seeing missionaries in their imperfections, encouraging them with the gospel, giving sacrificially, inviting others to participate, learning about other cultures, letting their kids join in, and leading the church in its heart for the nations? "The local church will be blessed...most importantly, God is glorified at the unity and functioning of the body responding to the headship of Jesus Christ in loving one another."[9]

Advocates await. And so do the sent ones who desperately need them.

---

[1] Bethlehem Baptist Church. (23 November 2012). *Sending to the Nations: Next Steps from Global Focus - Barnabas Support Teams.* Retrieved from http://www.hopeingod.org/news-events/bethlehem-blogs/global-outreach-blog/sending-nations-next-steps-global-focus-barnabas-su.

[2] The Austin Stone Community Church. *The Austin Stone 100 People Network: GOER Advocacy Team.* Retrieved from http://www.100peoplenetwork.org/wp-content/uploads/2014/01/Advocacy-Team-Description-and-Roles.pdf.

[3] Sojourn International. (2010). *Advocate Teams.* Retrieved from http://international.sojournchurch.com/?page_id=2525.

[4] College Park Church. (2014). *Get Involved with Global Outreach.* Retrieved from http://www.yourchurch.com/care-outreach/global-outreach/get-involved/.

[5] Tom Telford, *Today's All-Star Missions Churches: Strategies to Help Your Church Get Into the Game* (Grand Rapids, MI: Baker, 2001, 27.

[6] Rob Hay, Valerie Lim, Detlef Blocher, Jaap Ketelaar, and Sarah Hay, *Worth Keeping: Global Perspectives on Best Practice in Missionary Retention* (Pasadena, CA: William Carey Library, 2007), 374.

[7] Neal Pirolo, *Serving as Senders - Today* (San Diego, CA: Emmaus Road International, 2012), 16.

[8] Hay, Lim, Blocher, Ketelaar, and Hay, *Worth*, 375.

[9] Ibid., 375.

while making disciples

> A Sending Church is a local community of Christ-followers who have made a covenant together to be prayerful, deliberate, and proactive in developing, commissioning, and sending their own members both locally and globally, often in partnership with other churches or agencies, and continuing to encourage, support, and advocate for them **while making disciples** cross-culturally.

In the summer of 2014 the International Mission Board, the world's largest and perhaps most influential missions agency, made headlines when they announced (R)adical pastor David Platt as their new president. Despite some debate among Southern Baptists, the strategic move came as good news not solely for the 3 billion people who need missionaries mobilized among them, but for the 40,000 Southern Baptist churches who need fresh vision for taking the prominent role in that mobilization. On that note Platt himself said in an initial interview,

I want to take whatever influence the Lord has given me, and will give me in this position, to sound the trumpet among followers of Christ—Southern Baptists and non-Southern Baptists—to say that missions is not a compartmentalized program. The local church

is the agent God has promised to bless for the spread of the gospel to the nations. The role of the IMB is to equip and empower and encourage the local church to do that.[1]

The influence that Platt speaks of came in large part through his best-selling books *Radical*[2] and *Follow Me*[3], as well as his prolific teaching at national events such as *Together for the Gospel*[4] and *Secret Church*[5]. In each medium Platt essentially leverages a robust theological view of Christ to reframe and plead for a more biblical approach to discipleship, one that parts sharply with American tendencies toward selfishness and ease. Discipleship is defined as obedience to Christ, and obedience to Christ means mission both locally and globally. No Christian is excluded. For sending churches, this news was pretty rad (pun intended).

However, as sending church trends, the elements we've discussed in this book could easily become the mission in and of themselves. So we come to the finale of this project with a firm reminder of why sending matters: to make disciples of Jesus Christ. Sending church is not 'we're excited about missions' church. It's 'we're making disciples of Jesus Christ' church.

Where does that begin? Not necessarily in cross-cultural neighborhoods and nations. It starts with your people. Eric Wright notes that "the local church is where future missionaries are [made]."[6] On this point churches do well to heed the message of agencies such as Pioneers[7] and Serge[8], who are sensitive to the spiritual health of missionaries as first priority. Sent ones must love Jesus more than they love mission. Churches that desire to multiply missionaries are churches that lead their people to love Christ more than anything else. And we know, of course, this doesn't mean ambiguous feelings, but is measured by obedience to Christ's commands (John 14:15).

So here's the nuance. Disciples who love Jesus will also love his church. The time for Christians to pursue missionary service because they're dissatisfied with the church or because they "don't fit in" should be over. That doesn't mean that those who are passionate about cross-cultural mission should never be frustrated by churches who aren't passionate about cross-cultural mission. Jesus makes it clear that apathy in the church is *not ok* (see any part of Revelation 2-3). In reality, the church's imperfections bring disappointment for us all sometimes. The difference is in how we *respond* to the church. It's all about posture.

Consider the posture of Paul toward the church. I mean, he was the quintessential example of desiring to "preach the gospel, not where Christ [had] already been named" (Romans 15:20). Commissioned and gifted as the apostle to the Gentiles, he could have been vehemently tempted to see wayward, sluggish churches like Corinth as holding him back from the next frontier. Yet his passion for cross-cultural mission was never segregated from his devotion to the church. Indeed, he expected love (Philippians 4:10), prayer (Ephesians 6:19), and resources (Romans 15:25) from the churches for the advance of the mission. But he also sent love (Philippians 4:1), prayer (Ephesians 1:16), and resources (Colossians 4:8) back to the churches. And even if we were tempted at this point to say that Paul's concern for the church was only driven by his apostolic authority, George Peters observes that

he did not exercise such authority in missionary partnership. Here he was a humble brother and energetic leader among fellow laborers, and a dynamic and exemplary force in the churches in evangelism and church expansion.[9]

Paul was a model sent one not just for taking a posture of *reciprocation* toward the church, but *initiation*. He understood that "the Great Commission is a church-centered mandate," and that building *her* meant building the *kingdom*.[10]

What does this have to do with discipleship and the sending church? Before disciple-making ever crosses cultures, it begins by instructing believers with an appropriate posture toward Christ and his church. Like Paul, sent ones have the capacity to be "a dynamic and exemplary force" in encouraging their sending churches on mission. Think of the power of a missionary saying, "Pastor, how can I help you fulfill our church's mission?" Instead, many hold the privileged assumption that the church alone sends love, prayer, and resources. It's the job of the sending church to cast and cultivate a vision for reciprocation—and even initiation—from their sent ones.

With this kind of foundational discipleship in place, sending churches have a much a greater potential for the next step: making disciples *cross-culturally*.

[1] Erich Bridges. (28 August 2014). *2nd View: Pastor David Platt Succeeds Tom Elliff as IMB President*. Retrieved from http://www.bpnews.net/43249/2nd-view-pastor-david-platt-succeeds-tom-elliff-as-imb-president.

[2] David Platt, *Radical: Taking Back Your Faith From the American Dream* (Colorado Springs, CO: Multnomah, 2010).

[3] David Platt, *Follow Me: A Call to Die; A Call to Live* (Carol Stream, IL: Tyndale House Publishers, 2013).

[4] t4g.org

[5] http://www.radical.net/secretchurch/

[6] Eric C. Wright, *A Practical Theology of Missions: Dispelling the Mystery; Recovering the Passion* (Leominster, UK: Day One Publications, 2010), 228.

[7] Pioneers USA. *About Us: Pioneers Core Values*. Retrieved from http://www.pioneers.org/corevalues.

[8] World Harvest Mission. (2009). *Grow*. Retrieved from http://www.whm.org/grow.

[9] George W. Peters, *A Biblical Theology of Missions* (Chicago, IL: Moody Publishers, 1984), 236.

[10] Wright, *Theology*, 217.

cross-culturally

A Sending Church is a local community of Christ-followers who have made a covenant together to be prayerful, deliberate, and proactive in developing, commissioning, and sending their own members both locally and globally, often in partnership with other churches or agencies, and continuing to encourage, support, and advocate for them while making disciples **cross-culturally**.

So this is the end. We have arrived at the final phrase of the definition that's taken a book to even briefly hash out. And perhaps no part is more endemic to sending than "cross-culturally".

In John 20:21 Jesus said, "As the Father has sent me, even so I am sending you." Crossing cultures is the *nature* of mission. In Matthew 28:19 Jesus said, "Go therefore and make disciples of all nations". Crossing cultures is the *necessity* of mission. And in Matthew 24:14 he said, "this gospel of the kingdom will be proclaimed throughout the world as a testimony to all nations, and then the end will come." Crossing cultures is the *guarantee* of mission. Pretty plain and simple.

But if it's so apparent, why's it so difficult? Why do all churches tend toward outsourcing or abandoning cross-cultural mission altogether unless they are nourished with God's word, God's Spirit, and occasional doses of God's correction? This stiff-necked-ness is nothing new. In fact, church history is marked by resistance as much as obedience.

Keying off Kenneth Scott Latourette's monster text, *A History of Christianity*, missiologist Ralph Winter writes that church history—really the entire redemption narrative—displays a God zealous to fulfill his global mission through a pretty stubborn people. Winter even says that the church age isn't all that different from the Old Testament in that nations who do receive the blessing of knowing God over time grow less eager to share that blessing with others. Yet the Bible and history show God tenaciously propelling his glory among the nations both through his faithful and despite his unfaithful.[1]

Take the first three hundred years of Christianity, for example. The gospel epically moved from a cave in Bethlehem to a palace in Rome, the greatest empire the world had ever seen. Yet even with the face of Jesus still fresh in their minds, plus the newly-arrived Holy Spirit indwelling their hearts, Acts tells a story of the church being *nudged* across cultures. The movement remained widely stuck in Jerusalem until the persecution of Acts 8 forced believers into Judea and Samaria. It had been an almost entirely Jewish phenomenon until God jostled Peter awake and sent him to Cornelius in Acts 11. And without the appointment of Paul as the apostle to the Gentiles, who knows how long it would have taken to reap the harvest that awaited in gateway cities throughout the Roman empire. The faithful few took on great suffering to expand the gospel to places like North Africa, central Asia, and east Asia, while many believers crossed cultures only when they had to migrate. And yet by God's resilience Rome still became overwhelmingly Christian.[2]

However, as peace for the church settled in the Roman empire, so did the Christian burden for mission. There was no broad concern for the conversion of the barbarian hordes to the north. And without the influence of a church on mission, cultural decay buckled Rome under the conquering barbarians in the fifth century. The church was not completely wiped out, but suffered tremendously. And as it did, the gospel abounded among the Barbarians. Most of the church had chosen not to cross cultures with the gospel, but God made sure that it did anyway—albeit at great cost to his bride.[3]

This awkward dance of the nations raging, the majority of the church hesitating, and the gospel advancing can be traced on and on. The disinterested Barbarian church was conquered by the Vikings. The misguided Viking-ish Crusaders were conquered by war and plague. Catholic Europe tried to conquer Protestants and colonies, but effectively lost its grip on the gospel of grace. Just like the waves that brought them ashore, both the advance and the retreat of the church delivered the gospel to North America.[4] And even while

North American churches eased into a Christendom-like subcultured Christianity, the epicenter of gospel movement advanced to the Global South.[5]

As Jonathan Edwards concluded in *A History of the Work of Redemption*, God considers that his glory is lacking until he covers the earth with "the church, which is his body, the fullness of him who fills all in all" (Ephesians 1:22-23). So God spared himself no expense in the harnessing of the church, and he spares the church no expense in the harvesting of the nations. Scripture tells us that the gospel *will* advance across every culture in anticipation of the day that some from every nation, tribe, people, and language will be "standing before the throne and before the Lamb, clothed in white robes, with palm branches in their hands, and crying out with a loud voice, 'Salvation belongs to our God who sits on the throne, and to the Lamb!'"(Revelation 7:9-10)

Thus, may sending our people into cross-cultural neighborhoods and nations be more than a trend or an option—it's the very nature, necessity, and guarantee of God's redemptive plan! No doubt, being faithful as the church both locally *and* globally is a tall order, and only possible with God. So know up front that our human tendency will always be toward what's most immediate, familiar, self-serving, and easy. But God will accomplish his cross-cultural mission with or without the oscillating North American empire. For North American churches, that biting truth is both disturbing and

153

inviting. For churches who still have ears to hear, it's a call to send cross-culturally.[6]

[1] Ralph Winter and Steven C. Hawthorne, Eds., *Perspectives on the World Christian Movement* (Pasadena, CA: William Carey Library, 2013), 209-211.
[2] Ibid., 213-216.
[3] Ibid., 216-219.
[4] Ibid., 219-227,
[5] The Traveling Team. *The Global South: Ever Heard of Lafricasia?* Retrieved from http://www.thetravelingteam.org/stateworld/global-south.
[6] Jonathan K. Dodson. (9 April 2012). *Why the Missional Church Isn't Enough*. Retrieved from http://www.thegospelcoalition.org/article/why-the-missional-church-isnt-enough; I am indebted to Dodson's resourceful article in the writing of this chapter.

Conclusion

In a dark corner of an antique store's basement I recently came across a ratty copy of *Walking the Amazon*[1], which chronicles Ed Stafford's mad expedition to do just that—walk the entire length of the Amazon River. Fifty cents seemed like a reasonable price to get lost in a manly page-turner, so I picked up the volume. I was expecting *Indiana Jones* meets *Anaconda* meets David Livingstone. What I got was a read that felt as monotonous as the 860-day trudge through the jungle itself. Eclipsed by visa troubles, local suspicion, overweight gear, drug cartels, death threats, team conflict, and mosquito larva burrowed under his skin, Stafford spent most of his epic journey vacillating between depression, anger, and loneliness. Only at the end, with his tortured feet in the Atlantic Ocean and a Guinness World Record on his shoulders, did he rise from the gloom to overlook the historic feat. And even then his mind wandered toward the next big adventure.

What a picture of the challenge for anyone who lives in the part of redemption history that we call the church age! To us has been given the outrageous privilege of knowing this:

"the mystery that has been kept hidden for ages and generations, but is now disclosed to the Lord's people. To them God has chosen to make known among the Gentiles the glorious riches of this mystery, which is Christ in you, the hope of glory." (Colossians 1:26-27)

Consider afresh the manner of grace extended to us: in this age the Messiah is *knowable*—more than that, is *available*. In the grand scheme of things, what a time to be alive! Oh, how we fail to marvel that living in a post-Pentecost world means we can finally have all of God we want! Just like Stafford's journey, life and ministry with its burdens and distractions so easily entangles our hearts and minds. The empty tomb feels a million miles back and the second coming a million more ahead, and often all we can see in every direction is the very normal, very monotonous jungle of life and ministry. Our churches easily settle for less than the cosmic vision that God has for each of them.

This book is a plea to recognize the times. We have trumpeted the sending nature of God and the resulting sent identity of his people. The biblical evidence for sending every member into the neighborhoods and the nations demands a kind of ecclesiology and missiology that we have long forsaken. The desperation of this text is not to see "missions churches" abound, as if what our churches need is a new ministry affinity. Rather, we are crying out for the church to remember the fullness of *whose* it is and thus *who* it is. A prophetic word (think corrective, not predictive) always speaks to the times, and this is the time for the church to reclaim her birthright as the commissioned leader in the mission of Jesus Christ. This is what God has chosen for this chapter of his story. Let us not choose less.

Even in such a simple format we understand that the information given in this book can be overwhelming, especially for those of you just getting acquainted to the idea, those of you at small churches, and those of you at churches with years of mission malpractice. So here are a few basic next steps to help you practically move forward from wherever you are:

Pray

No really, start here. Many of the most significant mission movements in the New Testament and throughout church history have begun with a handful of people praying earnestly.[2] Gather a small group together regularly and commit to pray for your church to grow in mission. Use the Scriptures as a guide in what to pray for. Pray specifically for your pastor(s) and also that God would empower you and/or your group to model what you desire to see happen throughout the church.

Consult

Draw near to other churches who are already sending well. Ask them to tell you their story. It's ok to recreate some of what they do, but always keep your unique context in mind. Upstream partners with sending churches throughout the US to facilitate sending church roundtables. Attend one close to you to talk through some of the basics alongside other churches. Consider what your church already does well and how that plays into sending.

Collaborate

Once you get to know other sending churches in your area, get together occasionally as mission leaders to share ideas, successes, and struggles. This may even lead to partnering together. Upstream helps churches do this, and even provides info to facilitate discussion. We call them sending church cohorts.

Educate

Don't just consume information about the sending church. Pass it on. Encourage everyone on your staff to read this book, or walk a group through it chapter by chapter. Lead by asking good questions that cause people to reflect on why the church does what it does. Like a good missionary, contextualize these principles to your people so they can understand why it matters.

Practice

Start putting to work some of the things you're learning. Not just vision and systems, but being a sent one yourself. If you want your church to think and act like missionaries, then you think and act like a missionary. Pick up a copy of Upstream's book, *Tradecraft: For the Church on Mission*,[3] and practice each skill in your neighborhood.

Explore

As God quickens your heart toward people and places both locally and globally, go explore. Use some of the missionary tradecraft you've picked up, like prayer walking and mapping. Ask seasoned sending church leaders to go with you. Each year Upstream conducts Jet Set Trips all over the world for this very purpose, empowering churches to send strategically.

If you have walked through these basic steps, then you're laying a promising foundation in being a sending church. No two churches have the same journey. With great joy God is doing a unique work in your church that contributes to Jesus' grand mission. You've got a million miles to go. Take every step with him. With Paul I offer this expectant word:

Now to him who is able to do immeasurably more than all we ask or imagine, according to his power that is at work within us, to him be glory in the church and in Christ Jesus throughout all generations, forever and ever! Amen. (Ephesians 3:20-21)

[1] Ed Stafford, *Walking the Amazon: 860 Days, One Step at a Time* (New York, NY: Penguin, 2011).
[2] Citygate Films. (2014). *A Short History of Student Missions.* Retrieved at http://vimeo.com/82571012.
[3] Larry E. McCrary, Caleb Crider, Wade Stephens, and Rodney Calfee, *Tradecraft: For the Church on Mission* (Portland, OR: Urban Loft Publishers, 2013).

Bibliography

Adeney, Miriam. *Kingdom Without Borders: The Untold Story of Global Christianity*. Downers Grove, IL: IVP Books, 2009.

Alexander, Desmond T. *From Eden to the New Jerusalem: An Introduction to Biblical Theology*. Grand Rapids, MI: Kregel Academic, 2009.

Allen, Roland. *Missionary Methods: St. Paul's or Ours?* Seattle: CreateSpace, 2012.

Allen, Rolland. *Missionary Principles—and Practice*. Cambridge, UK: Lutterworth Press, 2006.

Allen, Roland. *The Spontaneous Expansion of the Church: And the Causes That Hinder It*. Eugene, OR: Wifp and Stock Publishers, 1962.

Allison, Gregg R. *Sojourners and Strangers: The Doctrine of the Church*. Wheaton, IL: Crossway, 2012.

Anyabwile, Thabiti. 18 March 2014. *Being a Missions-Centered Local Church: Lessons from Johnson Ferry Baptist Church*. Retrieved from http://www.thegospelcoalition.org/blogs/thabitianyabwile/2014/03/18/being-a-missions-centered-local-church-lessons-from-johnson-ferry-baptist-church/.

Ashford, Bruce Riley, ed. *Theology and Practice of Mission: God, the Church, and the Nations*. Nashville, TN: B&H Academic, 2011.

Associated Press. 5 August 2014. *American Missionary with Ebola En Route to US*. Retrieved from http://nypost.com/2014/08/05/american-missionary-infected-with-ebola-en-route-to-us/.

Back to Jerusalem. 22 August 2013. *BTJ Missionaries in Syria*. Retrieved from https://backtojerusalem.com/v3/2013/08/btj-missionaries-in-syria/

Band of Brothers. "Points". Directed by Mikael Salomon. USA: DreamWorks, 2001.

Barna, George. *Revolution: Finding Vibrant Faith Beyond the Walls of the Sanctuary.* Carol Stream, IL: Tyndale Momentum, 2012.

Barnett, Mike, ed. *Discovering the Mission of God: Best Missional Practices for the 21st Century.* Downers Grove, IL: IVP Academic, 2012.

Beals, Paul A. *A People for His Name: A Church-Based Missions Strategy.* Pasadena, CA: William Carey Library, 2013.

Belcher, Jim. *Deep Church: A Third Way Beyond Emerging and Traditional.* Downers Grove, IL: IVP Books, 2009.

Bethlehem Baptist Church. 23 November 2012. *Sending to the Nations: Next Steps from Global Focus - Barnabas Support Teams.* Retrieved from http://www.hopeingod.org/news-events/bethlehem-blogs/global-outreach-blog/sending-nations-next-steps-global-focus-barnabas-su.

Blomberg, Craig L. *From Pentecost to Patmos: An Introduction to Acts through Revelation.* Nashville, TN: B&H Academic, 2006.

Boice, James Montgomery. *Acts: An Expositional Commentary.* Grand Rapids, MI: Baker, 2006.

Bonhoeffer, Dietrich, *Life Together.* New York, NY: HarperOne, 2009.

Bonhoeffer, Dietrich. *Meditations on the Cross.* Louisville, KY: Westminster John Knox Press, 1998.

Bonhoeffer, Dietrich. *The Cost of Discipleship.* New York, NY: Simon and Schuster, 1959.

Borthwick, Paul. *Western Christians in Global Mission: What's the Role of the North American Church?* Downers Grove: IVP Books, 2012.

Bosch, David J. *Transforming Mission: Paradigm Shifts in Theology of Mission.* Maryknoll, NY: Orbis Books, 2011.

Bounds, E. M. *The Complete Works of E. M. Bounds on Prayer.* Grand Rapids, MI: Baker, 1990.

Bradley, Zach. 16 December 2013. *Blood on Both Ends of the Rope: A Broader Definition of the Sending Church.* Retrieved from http://international.sojournchurch.com/?p=4416.

Bridges, Erich. 28 August 2014. *2nd View: Pastor David Platt Succeeds Tom Elliff as IMB President.* Retrieved from http://www.bpnews.net/43249/2nd-view-pastor-david-platt-succeeds-tom-elliff-as-imb-president.

Calvin, John. *Acts.* Wheaton, IL: Crossway, 1995.

Carey, William. *An Enquiry into the Obligations of Christians, to Use Means for the Conversion of the Heathens.* Leicester: Anne Ireland, 1792.

CBS News. 19 December 2013. *Widow of American Teacher Shot in Libya Says She Forgives Husband's Attackers.* Retrieved from http://www.cbsnews.com/news/widow-of-american-teacher-shot-in-libya-says-she-forgives-husbands-attackers/.

Carlson, Darren. 10 June 2012. *Celebrating the Short-Term Missions Boom.* Retrieved from http://www.thegospelcoalition.org/article/celebrating-the-short-term-missions-boom/.

Carlson, Darren. 27 June 2012. *Toward Better Short-Term Missions.* Retrieved from http://www.thegospelcoalition.org/article/toward-better-short-term-missions/.

Carson, D. A. *A Call to Spiritual Reformation: Priorities from Paul and His Prayers.* Grand Rapids, MI: Baker Academic, 1992.

Carter, Greg. *Skills, Knowledge, Character: A Church-Based Approach to Missionary Candidate Preparation.* Valparaiso, IN: Turtle River Press, 2010.

Chandler, Matt, Mike McKinley, and Jonathan Leeman. 2013. *Membership and Mission: Why Membership Matters for the Church's Mission.* Retrieved from http://resources.thegospelcoalition.org/library/membership-and-mission-why-membership-matters-for-the-church-s-mission-9marks-panel-discussion-mike-mckinley-jonathan-leeman.

Cheong, Robert K. *God Redeeming His Bride: A Handbook for Church Discipline.* Scotland, UK: Christian Focus Publications, 2013.

Chester, Tim and Steve Timmis. *Everyday Church: Gospel Communities on Mission*. Wheaton, IL: Crossway, 2012.

Chester, Tim and Steve Timmis. *Total Church: A Radical Reshaping Around Gospel and Community*. Wheaton, IL: Crossway, 2008.

Citygate Films. 2014. *A Short History of Student Missions*. Retrieved at http://vimeo.com/82571012.

College Park Church. 2014. *Get Involved with Global Outreach*. Retrieved from http://www.yourchurch.com/care-outreach/global-outreach/get-involved/.

Conn, Harvie M. and Manuel Ortiz. *Urban Ministry: The Kingdom, the City, and the People of God*. Downers Grove, IL: IVP Academic, 2010.

Corbett, Steve and Brian Fikkert. *When Helping Hurts: How to Alleviate Poverty Without Hurting the Poor...and Yourself*. Chicago, IL: Moody Publishers, 2014.

Cosper, Mike. 5 February 2014. *Donald Miller and the Culture of Contemporary Worship*. Retrieved from http://www.mikedcosper.com/home/donald-miller-and-the-culture-of-contemporary-worship.

Cosper, Mike. *Rhythms of Grace: How the Church's Worship Tells the Story of the Gospel*. Wheaton, IL: Crossway, 2013.

Cross Conference. 2014. *Panel with John Piper and Mark Dever*. Retrieved from crosscon.com/media/2013/12/cross-2013-panel-with-john-piper-and-mark-dever/.

Dever, Mark. *Nine Marks of a Healthy Church*. Wheaton, IL: Crossway, 2013.

DeYoung, Kevin. 2013. *Five Surprising Motivations for Missions*. Retrieved from http://crosscon.com/media/2014/01/five-surprising-motivations-for-mission-session-iii/.

DeYoung, Kevin and Greg Gilbert. *What is the Mission of the Church? Making Sense of Shalom, Social Justice, and the Great Commission*. Wheaton, IL: Crossway, 2011.

Dodson, Jonathan K. 9 April 2012. *Why the Missional Church Isn't Enough*. Retrieved from http://www.thegospelcoalition.org/article/why-the-missional-church-isnt-enough.

Dukes, Jason C. *Live Sent: You Are A Letter*. Birmingham, AL: New Hope Publishers, 2011.

Edwards, Jonathan. *A Treatise on Religious Affections*. Grand Rapids, MI: Baker, 1982.

Eenigenburg, Sue and Robynn Bliss. *Expectations and Burnout: Women Surviving the Great Commission*. Elizabethton, TN: William Carey Library, 2010.

Elmer, Duane. *Cross-Cultural Servanthood: Serving the World in Christlike Humility*. Downers Grove, IL: IVP Books, 2006.

Frame, John. *Systematic Theology: An Introduction to Christian Belief*. Philipsburg, NJ: P&R Publishing, 2013.

Garth, Nathan. *Sojourn International Mission Convictions*. Retrieved from http://theupstreamcollective.org/wp-content/uploads/2011/11/MISSION-CONVICTIONS-Sojourn-.pdf.

Gilbert, Greg. *What is the Gospel?* Wheaton, IL: Crossway, 2010.

Goen, Kyle. 21 July 2014. *with other churches or agencies, part 3*. Retrieved from http://theupstreamcollective.org/2014/07/21/with-other-churches-or-agencies-part-3/.

Goulding, Verdell. 2014. "Voices in the Local Church: A Passion for Souls: Our Continued Journey in Global Missions". *Evangelical Missions Quarterly*, vol. 50, no. 1.

Hale, Thomas. *On Being a Missionary*. Pasadena, CA: William Carey Library, 2012.

Harley, David. *Preparing to Serve: Training for Cross-Cultural Mission*. Pasadena, CA: William Carey Library, 2012.

Hastings, Ross. *Missional God, Missional Church: Hope for Re-Evangelizing the West*. Downers Grove, IL: IVP Academic, 2012.

Hay, Rob, Valerie Lim, Detlef Blocher, Jaap Ketelaar, and Sarah Hay. *Worth Keeping: Global Perspectives on Best Practice in Missionary Retention.* Elizabethton, TN: William Carey Library, 2013.

Haynes, Brian. *Shift: What it Takes to Finally Reach Families Today.* Loveland, CO: Group Publishing, 2009.

Hesselgrave, David J. *Paradigms in Conflict: 10 Key Questions in Christian Missions Today.* Grand Rapids, MI: Kregel Academic, 2005.

Hiebert, Paul G. *Anthropological Insights for Missionaries.* Grand Rapids, MI: Baker Academic, 1986.

Hood, Pat. *The Sending Church: The Church Must Leave the Building.* Nashville, TN: B&H Books, 2013.

Horner, David. *Firmly Rooted, Faithfully Growing: Principle-Based Ministry in the Church.* Raleigh, NC: Providence Communications, 2003.

Horner, David. *When Missions Shapes the Mission: You and Your Church Can Reach the World.* Nashville, TN: B&H Books, 2011.

Horton, Michael S. *People and Place: A Covenant Ecclesiology.* Louisville, KY: Westminster John Knox, 2008.

House, Brad. *Community: Taking Your Small Group Off Life Support.* Wheaton, IL: Crossway, 2011.

Howell, Clifford G. *The Advanced Guard of Missions.* Mountain View, CA: Pacific Press Publishing, 1912.

Hughes, R. Kent. *Acts: The Church Afire.* Wheaton, IL: Crossway, 1996.

Hybels, Bill. *Too Busy Not to Pray.* Downers Grove, IL: IVP Books, 2008.

Jenkins, Philip. *The Next Christendom: The Coming of Global Christianity.* Oxford: Oxford Press, 2002.

Jerajani, H. R., Bhagyashri Jaju, M. M. Phiske, and Nitin Lade. July-September 2009. *Hematohidrosis: A Rare Clinical Phenomenon.* Retrieved from http://www.ncbi.nlm.nih.gov/pmc/articles/PMC2810702/.

166

Johnstone, Patrick. *The Future of the Global Church: History, Trends, and Possibilities.* Downers Grove, IL: IVP Books, 2011.

Jones, Robert P., Daniel Cox, and Juhem Navarro-Rivera. 26 February 2014. *A Shifting Landscape.* Retrieved from http://publicreligion.org/site/wp-content/uploads/2014/02/2014.LGBT_REPORT.pdf?utm_source=Albert+Mohler&utm_campaign=c7b98e7d9c-The_Briefing_2013&utm_medium=email&utm_term=0_b041ba0d12-c7b98e7d9c-307182206.

Jones, Timothy Paul. *Family Ministry Field Guide: How Your Church Can Equip Parents to Make Disciples.* Indianapolis, IN: Wesleyan Publishing House, 2011.

Keller, Timothy J. *Center Church: Doing Balanced, Gospel-Centered Ministry in Your City.* Grand Rapids, MI: Zondervan, 2012.

Keller, Timothy J. *Ministries of Mercy: The Call of the Jericho Road.* Philipsburg, NJ: P&R Publishing, 1997.

Kimball, Dan. *They Like Jesus But Not the Church: Insights from Emerging Generations.* Grand Rapids, MI: Zondervan, 2007.

Knell, Marion. *Burn-Up or Splash Down: Surviving the Culture Shock of Re-Entry.* Downers Grove, IL: IVP Books, 2007.

Kostenberger, Andreas J. *Salvation to the Ends of the Earth: A Biblical Theology of Mission.* Downers Grove, IL: IVP Academic, 2001.

Lederleitner, Mary T. *Cross-Cultural Partnership: Navigating the Complexities of Money and Mission.* Downers Grove, IL: IVP Books, 2010.

Leeman, Jonathan *Church Membership: How the World Knows Who Represents Jesus.* Wheaton, IL: Crossway, 2012.

Lewis, C. S. *The Weight of Glory.* New York, NY: HarperCollins, 2001.

Livermore, David A. *Cultural Intelligence: Improving Your CQ to Engage Our Multicultural World.* Grand Rapids, MI: Baker Academic, 2009.

Long, Justin. 6 July 2011. *75% Leave the Field in the First 3 Years, Never Return? It's a Myth—Sort Of.* Retrieved from http://www.justinlong.org/2011/07/75-leave-the-field-in-the-first-3-years-never-return-its-a-myth-sort-of/.

Luttrell, Marcus and Patrick Robinson. *Lone Survivor: The Eyewitness Account of Operation Redwing and the Lost Heroes of SEAL Team 10.* New York, NY: Back Bay Books, 2007.

Mandryk, Jason. *Operation World: The Definitive Prayer Guide to Every Nation.* Downers Grove, IL: IVP Books, 2010.

McCrary, Larry, Caleb Crider, Wade Stephens and Rodney Calfee. *Tradecraft: For the Church on Mission.* Portland, OR: Urban Loft Publishers, 2013.

McCrary, Larry. *The Sending Process.* Retrieved from http://theupstreamcollective.org/media/Sending_Assessment.pdf.

Merriam-Webster Dictionary. 2014. *Proactive.* Retrieved from http://www.merriam-webster.com/dictionary/proactive.

Miley, George. *Loving the Church, Blessing the Nations: Pursuing the Role of Local Churches in Global Mission.* Downers Grove, IL: IVP Books, 2005.

Miller, Donald. 3 February 2014. *I Don't Worship God By Singing. I Connect With Him Elsewhere.* Retrieved from http://storylineblog.com/2014/02/03/i-dont-worship-god-by-singing-i-connect-with-him-elsewhere/.

Miller, Donald. 5 February 2014. *Why I Don't Go to Church Very Often, A Follow Up.* Retrieved from http://storylineblog.com/2014/02/05/why-i-dont-go-to-church-very-often-a-follow-up-blog/.

Mohler, Jr., R. Albert. 13 February 2014. *Monotheism is Not Enough.* Retrieved from http://www.sbts.edu/resources/chapel/monotheism-is-not-enough/.

Montgomery, Daniel and Mike Cosper. *Faithmapping: A Gospel Atlas for Your Spiritual Journey.* Wheaton, IL: Crossway, 2013.

Montgomery, Daniel. 19 January 2014. *State of Communion.* Retrieved from http://sojournchurch.com/sermons/state-of-communion/.

Moreau, A. Scott. *Contextualization in World Missions: Mapping and Assessing Evangelical Models*. Grand Rapids, MI: Kregel Publications, 2012.

Moss, Tony. 18 March 2014. *Ranking the NCAA Tournament Coaches by Playing Career*, 1-68. Retrieved from http://www.cbssports.com/collegebasketball/eye-on-college-basketball/24490175/ranking-the-ncaa-tournament-coaches-by-playing-career-1-68.

Newbigin, Lesslie. *The Open Secret: An Introduction to the Theology of Mission*. Grand Rapids, MI: Eerdmans, 1995.

New Republic. 21 April 2014. *Earth Day: 'Think Globally, Act Locally' is Back*. Retrieved from http://www.newrepublic.com/article/117459/earth-day-2014-think-globally-act-locally-back.

Noll, Mark A. *Turning Points: Decisive Moments in the History of Christianity*. Grand Rapids, MI: Baker Academic, 2012.

Norman, R. Stanton, ed. The Mission of Today's Church: Baptist Leaders Look at Modern Faith Issues. Nashville, TN: B&H Publishing, 2013.
O'Donnell, Kelly. *Missionary Care: Counting the Cost for World Evangelization*. Elizabethton, TN: William Carey Library, 1999.

Ogne, Steve and Tim Roehl. *Transformissional Coaching: Empowering Leaders in a Changing Ministry World*. Nashville, TN: B&H Books, 2008.

Olson, Bruce. *Bruchko*. Lake Mary, FL: Charisma House, 1977.

Ott, Craig and Gene Wilson. *Global Church Planting: Biblical Principles and Best Practices for Multiplication*. Grand Rapids, MI: Baker Academic, 2011.

Ott, Craig, Stephen J. Strauss, and Timothy C. Tennent. *Encountering Theology of Missions: Biblical Foundations, Historical Developments, and Contemporary Issues*. Grand Rapids, MI: Baker Academic, 2010.

Paton, John Gibson. *The Story of John G. Paton Or Thirty Years Among South Sea Cannibals*. New York, NY: A.L. Burton Company, 1892. Kindle edition.

Patra, Kevin. 26 January 2014. *Team Rice Defeats Team Sanders in NFL Pro Bowl.* Retrieved from www.nfl.com/news/story/0ap2000000318206/article/team-rice-defeats-team-sanders-in-nfl-pro-bowl.

Payne, J. D. *Pressure Points: Twelve Global Issues Shaping the Face of the Church.* Nashville, TN: Thomas Nelson, 2013.

Perman, Matt. *What's Best Next: How the Gospel Transforms the Way You Get Things Done.* Grand Rapids, MI: Zondervan, 2014.

Perry, Tobin. 15 August 2014. *St. Louis Planters Organize Ferguson Cleanup.* Retrieved from http://www.namb.net/nambblogSt.Louis.aspx?id=12884911351&blogid=8590116839.

Peters, George W. *A Biblical Theology of Missions.* Chicago, IL: Moody, 1984.

Pioneers USA. *About Us: Pioneers Core Values.* Retrieved from http://www.pioneers.org/corevalues.

Pioneers USA. *Church Partners.* Retrieved from http://www.pioneers.org/Send/ChurchPartners.aspx.

Piper, John. *Andrew Fuller: I Will Go Down If You Will Hold the Rope!* Minneapolis, MN: Desiring God, 2012.

Piper, John. 31 October 1984. *A Pastor's Role in World Missions.* Retrieved from http://www.desiringgod.org/conference-messages/a-pastors-role-in-world-missions.

Piper, John. 13 February 2011. *Don't Waste Your Retirement.* Retrieved from https://www.youtube.com/watch?v=mSl_SCQkaYg.

Piper, John. 24 June 2011. *Goers, Senders, and the Disobedient.* Retrieved from http://www.desiringgod.org/interviews/goers-senders-and-the-disobedient.

Piper, John. *Let the Nations Be Glad: The Supremacy of God in Missions.* Grand Rapids, MI: Baker Academic, 2010.

Piper, John. 25 November 1991. *Soundbites from the Battlefield.* Retrieved from http://www.desiringgod.org/articles/soundbites-from-the-battlefield.

Piper, John. 4 January 2007. *The Power to Risk in the Cause of Christ.* Retrieved from http://www.desiringgod.org/conference-messages/the-power-to-risk-in-the-cause-of-christ.

Pirolo, Neal. *Serving as Senders.* San Diego, CA: Emmaus Road International, 1991.

Pirolo, Neal. *Serving as Senders - Today.* San Diego, CA: Emmaus Road International, 2012.

Pirolo, Neal. *The Reentry Team: Caring for Your Returning Missionaries.* San Diego, CA: Emmaus Road International, 2000.

Platt, David. *Follow Me: A Call to Die, A Call to Live.* Carol Stream, IL: Tyndale House Publishers, 2013.

Platt, David. *Radical: Taking Back Your Faith From the American Dream.* Colorado Springs, CO: Multnomah, 2010.

Plummer, Robert L. and John Mark Terry, ed. *Paul's Missionary Methods: In His Time and Ours.* Downers Grove, IL: IVP Academic, 2012.

Pocock, Michael, Gailyn van Rheenen, and Douglas McConnell. *The Changing Face of Missions: Engaging Contemporary Issues and Trends.* Grand Rapids, MI: Baker Academic, 2005.

Pollock, David C. and Ruth E. Van Reken. *Third Culture Kids: Growing Up Among Worlds.* Boston, MA: Nicholas Brealey Publishing, 2009.

Propempo International. 2013. *Get Over There! Get Your Church to Celebrate and Send You Out.* Retrieved from http://cross.propempo.com/8-get-over-there.html.

Pope, Randy. *The Intentional Church: Moving from Church Success to Community Transformation.* Chicago, IL: Moody Publishers, 2006.

Pratt, Zane, M. David Sills, and Jeff K. Walters. *Introduction to Global Missions.* Nashville, TN: B&H Academic, 2014.

Rankin, Jerry. *To the Ends of the Earth: Churches Fulfilling the Great Commission.* Richmond, VA: International Mission Board, 2005.

Rees, Jennie. 5 May 2014. *Kentucky Derby: California Chrome Shines Bright.* Retrieved from http://www.courier-journal.com/story/sports/horses/triple/derby/2014/05/03/kentucky-derby/8659903/.

Reeves, Michael. *Delighting in the Trinity: An Introduction to Christian Faith.* Downers Grove, IL: IVP, 2012.

Richards, E. Randolph and Brandon J. O'Brien. *Misreading Scripture with Western Eyes: Removing Cultural Blindness to Better Understand the Bible.* Downers Grove: IL, IVP Books, 2012.

Ripken, Nik. 20 October 2013. *A Present Tense Resurrection.* Retrieved from http://east.sojournchurch.com/sermons/a-present-tense-resurrection-nik-ripken/.

Ripken, Nik. *The Insanity of God: A True Story of Faith Resurrected.* Nashville, TN: B&H Books, 2013.

Roxburgh, Alan and Fred Romanuk. *The Missional Leader: Equipping Your Church to Reach a Changing World.* Indianapolis, IN: Jossey-Bass, 2006.

Ryken, Philip Graham. *Luke.* Philipsburg, NJ: P&R Publishing, 2009.

SBC of Virginia. 13 December 2011. *About the Acts 1:8 Network.* Retrieved from http://www.sbcv.org/articles/detail/about_the_acts_18_network.

Schnabel, Eckhard J. *Paul the Missionary: Realities, Strategies, and Methods.* Downers Grove, IL: IVP Academic, 2008.

SEED. 2013. *About.* Retrieved from http://seed.sojournchurch.com/about-us/.

Sills, M. David. *Reaching and Teaching: A Call to Great Commission Obedience.* Chicago, IL: Moody Publishers, 2010.

Sills, M. David. *The Missionary Call: Find Your Place in God's Plan for the World.* Chicago, IL: Moody Publishers, 2008.

Sojourn Community Church. *Our Story and Our Name.* Retrieved from http://sojournchurch.com/about-us/our-story-and-our-name/.

Sojourn International. 2010. *Advocate Teams.* Retrieved from http://international.sojournchurch.com/?page_id=2525.

172

Sojourn International. 2010. *Self-Assessment*. Retrieved from http://international.sojournchurch.com/?page_id=4443.

Sojourn Music. 20 November 2012. *Come Ye Sinners*. Retrieved from http://sojournmusic.bandcamp.com/track/come-ye-sinners.

Sojourn Music. 20 November 2012. *The Day the Sky Went Black*. Retrieved from https://sojournmusic.bandcamp.com/track/the-day-the-sky-went-black.

Spurgeon, C. H. 31 August 1856. *Christ in the Covenant*. Retrieved from http://www.spurgeon.org/sermons/0103.htm.

Stafford, Ed. *Walking the Amazon: 860 Days, One Step at a Time*. New York, NY: Penguin, 2011.

Stephan, Melissa. 25 July 2013. *The Surprising Countries Most Missionaries are Sent From and Go To*. Retrieved from http://www.christianitytoday.com/gleanings/2013/july/missionaries-countries-sent-received-csgc-gordon-conwell.html?paging=off.

Stetzer, Ed. *Planting Missional Churches: Planting a Church That's Biblically Sound ad Reaching People in Culture*. Nashville, TN: B&H Academic, 2006.

Stinson, Randy and Timothy Paul Jones, ed. *Trained in the Fear of God: Family Ministry in Theological, Historical, and Practical Perspective*. Grand Rapids, MI: Kregel Academic, 2011.

Stott, John. *Basic Christianity*. Grand Rapids, MI: Eerdmans, 2012.

Stott, John R. W. *The Epistles of John*. Grand Rapids, MI: Eerdmans, 1988.

Taylor, Kate. 8 August 2014. *Indy Native with Ebola Releases Statement*. Retrieved from http://wishtv.com/2014/08/08/indy-native-with-ebola-releases-statement/

Taylor, William. *Too Valuable to Lose: Exploring the Causes and Cures of Missionary Attrition*. Elizabethton, TN: William Carey Library, 1997.

Telford, Tom. *Today's All-Star Missions Churches: Strategies to Help Your Church Get Into the Game.* Grand Rapids, MI: Baker Books, 2001.

The Austin Stone Community Church. *Partnership at The Austin Stone.* Retrieved from http://austinstone.org/connect/partnership.

The Austin Stone Community Church. *The Austin Stone 100 People Network: GOER Advocacy Team.* Retrieved from http://www. 100peoplenetwork.org/wp-content/uploads/2014/01/Advocacy-Team-Description-and-Roles.pdf.

The Economist Online. 29 December 2010. *Debt Forgetfulness.* Retrieved from http://www.economist.com/node/17800215.

The Economist Online. 4 July 2011. *Military Conscription: Does Your Country Need You?* Retrieved from www.economist.com/blogs/dailychart/2011/07/military-conscription.

The Princess Bride. Directed by Rob Reiner. USA: Acts III Communications, 1987.

The Traveling Team. *The Global South: Ever Heard of Lafricasia?* Retrieved from http://www.thetravelingteam.org/stateworld/global-south.

The Washington Post. 14 April 2014. *Google buys drone maker Titan Aerospace.* Retrieved from http://www.washingtonpost.com/blogs/the-switch/wp/2014/04/14/google-buys-drone-maker-titan-aerospace-2/.

Thomas, Scott and Tom Wood. *Gospel Coach: Shepherding Leaders to Glorify God.* Grand Rapids, MI: Zondervan, 2012.

Tucker, Ruth A. *From Jerusalem to Irian Jaya: A Biographical History of Christian Missions.* Grand Rapids, MI: Zondervan, 2004.

Ware, Bruce A. *Father, Son, and Holy Spirit: Relationships, Roles, and Relevance.* Wheaton, IL: Crossway, 2005.

Whitney, Donald S. *Spiritual Disciplines Within the Church: Participating Fully in the Body of Christ.* Chicago, IL: Moody, 1996.

Wilensky, Harold L. "The Professionalization of Everyone?" American Journal of Sociology. Issue 70. 1964. Print.

Willard, Dallas. *Hearing God: Developing a Conversational Relationship with God*. Downers Grove, IL: IVP Books, 1999.

Winter, Ralph D. *Perspectives on the World Christian Movement: A Reader, Third Ed*. Pasadena, CA: William Carey Library, 1999.

Winter, Ralph and Steven C. Hawthorne, eds., *Perspectives on the World Christian Movement*. Pasadena, CA: William Carey Library, 2013.

World Harvest Mission. 2009. Grow. Retrieved from http://www.whm.org/grow.

Wright, Christopher J. H. *The Mission of God's People: A Biblical Theology of the Church's Mission*. Grand Rapids, MI: Zondervan, 2010.

Wright, Christopher J. H. *The Mission of God: Unlocking the Bible's Grand Narrative*. Downers Grove, IL: IVP Academic, 2013.

Wright, Eric E. *A Practical Theology of Missions: Dispelling the Mystery; Recovering the Passion*. Leominster, UK: Day One Publications, 2010.

YouTube. 14 February 2007. *Mortal Kombat 1 Fatalities*. Retrieved from https://www.youtube.com/watch?v=BPyIK_Vnbl4.

Made in the USA
Lexington, KY
24 October 2019